# FORMULA 449 SUPERINTELLIGENCE SYNCHRONIZE

MICHAEL OLIVER

ISBN 978-1-961017-62-7 (Paperback)
ISBN 978-1-961017-63-4 (Ebook)


Inquiries and Book Orders should be addressed to:

Leavitt Peak Press
17901 Pioneer Blvd Ste L #298, Artesia, California 90701
Phone #: 2092191548

When Planets Dream in Love Mode

A Planet Upgrade to Human's Finest Life span

"Spend Time in the New Paradise Planet System"

New Philosophies Satisfy Time's True Intelligence,
Metaphorically Analogizing Your Space

Michael Oliver

All eyes on the human species, who currently are being hosted, cradled, and cared for by the magnificent planet called by the name Earth. She is now mature enough for sharing her time and space, for better or for worse, with the farms of lives she was destined to mother and raise in her sacred time and space. It is the holiest of matrimony, sacred and true to the destiny of the human species. Through time, they all came because time is the vehicle that delivered all life forms on that planet and all the planets in this universe. Time constant and forever giveth and taketh away all things and all life.

On that ever-faithful, always providing planet Earth, humans are the most dominant life form. A minor significance to the fact that humans find themselves still in a primitive state of life. Still the adolescent in the life span of their existence on the enormous wings of time, humans are becoming increasingly aware of their mortality, discovering the very important facts that all lifeforms share on planet Earth or elsewhere that every living thing—from very large to very tiny—has an average life span., starting from a few weeks to the vast numbers of trillions of years and all the numbers in between.

As planet Earth claim her place on the enormous ever-expanding planes of time and space, humans find themselves as a mere speck in that time and space, barely visible, with only the average life span of about eighty years as individual and a lifetime of a few million years as species. It takes an average of one hundred years to change the course of the human conditions by evolving the human knowledge that is all hidden in time.

Every species on that planet has their own average life span. Human's life span is among the longest on that planet. In the arena of time and space, all living things must conform to that space and that time including planets themselves. The average life span of planets is in the billions of years and galaxy systems in the trillions of years. It's difficult for most humans to perceive and/or come to term with time frames that are billions and trillions of years, going in or out of time. Because their life span is just a mere eighty-year average, they are more inclined to deal with the small fragments of time closest to their existence.

As human nature determined their behaviors, time brings the human species greater wisdom, knowledge, and technology as each generation constantly modifies their lifestyle and behaviors toward one another and their environment. The wisest among each species work diligently to enhance each moment for better future moments. They use the knowledge that they have acquired from experience wherever time finds them in that moment. Time delivers the wisdom that produces greater knowledge which make for higher intelligence. Through experience, there's always a great deal of knowledge yet to be discovered.

While humans work with what they have discovered so far, there is an abundance of greater, enhanced knowledge and technology just patiently waiting, anxious to be discovered—intel that could make life on that planet Earth so much easier, socially hospitable, more maneuverable, and pleasant, enhancing the quality of life, making the state of the human species' living conditions more satisfying for all of them and everything they encounter. One such knowledge that humans has not fully embraced yet is the fact that they all need one another for better survival on that planet Earth. The more they are together, the stronger, wiser, safer, happier, and more efficient they will all be.

Naturally embedded in the human's nature is the overwhelming need to be connected to one another socially, emotionally, physically, and psychologically. All those natural needs drive their daily task to become deeply connected and more emotionally and physically satisfied. The human species are slowly discovering that knowledge, the improved technology, that would be the vehicle that transports them into a new and more perfect union with one another on their planet Earth. It's almost an unbearable tragedy to watch the human species while they struggle to find the right ways to properly inhabit their super planet. They don't realize yet they're using time in the most primitive of ways, existing without evolving the most revolutionary knowledge—the kind that will lead them to the technologies that was given to them as their birthright.

This miraculous understanding of human life is now patiently awaiting the arrival of a highly intelligent generation of the human species. To become mature enough and advanced enough to claim and utilize their overall and all in "ONE" citizenship on that majestic planet. Technology that was hidden from past human generations is now revealed. What was hidden from the wise and prudent is now revealed to their offsprings. Time is the one that will unlock the true meaning of life for humans on that planet. Time is the ever-faithful hostess of all life spans on planet Earth. Time will be the one that will gently inform humans of the true meaning of their existence on planet Earth.

The true meaning of life for all humans and every living thing on planet earth "is to serve one and all in love, truth, and right, with an honest heart and a clear mind." When the human knowledge is mature enough to live in a synchronized partnership with this understanding, the human species will be then claiming their true place as the first most privileged super-intelligent species, accepting their dominion in good stewardship over all other life form on that planet. Their fullest potential lies in the ability to assume this responsibility with wisdom—the true and sacred wisdom that is locked in a relentless pursuit of better ways to govern themselves and all the life forms on that planet through the sacred principles of truth and righteousness, which are perfectly designed sets of morals and values that modified behaviors deeply seated in the human species' psychological, emotional, and physical makeup. Mostly microbic, these miracles of life, space, and time constantly function in the human's conscious and subconscious mind.

The mind is the most powerful thing that every living species on earth possesses. This is especially true for humans. The mind is the most meaningful conscious and subconscious connection to the truth—God, the creator of all life. The mind is humans' most powerful manufacture of all thoughts, without perimeters, with the means to produce everything—the intelligent ideas the human species can imagine and conceive for better advance, good, safe, and free-living condition. They all deserve the best life on their one-of-a-kind planet in all time. There is an incredible and miraculous amount of knowledge out on that planet just awaiting the time to bless humans with their true intelligence—the inheritance that was promised to them from the beginning of their time in that space.

The lack of knowledge is a huge obstacle that haunt and hail humans and their quality of life. This obstacle will finally be past in time, paving the way to humans living in paradise times, more in tune with their real self, near, dear, and true to the heart and soul of their humanity. The true birthright that once was hidden but now in this time is revealed and taught to the minds of the human species. This intelligence will naturally open the eyes and hearts of humans to finally submit to true super love for one another.

When humans study, acknowledge, and practice the true love that love one another as they love themselves, they will all reap the fruits of the love they sow. Their knowledge will vastly increase, and their living conditions will be upgraded, leaping forward to better times where they will not want for anything on that planet for their entire life spans—the life spans in times when truth is preferred to accompany their days, tightly embracing philosophies that is born of their true nature, morals, and values, rooted in serving and protecting one another forever, a time where unification prevails, and they finally realize the facts of life.

The true meaning of their species life on that planet is to serve one another. Their minds are now in a heightened awareness of their true self. Now their tongues are confessing to one another the truths of a more abundant life. The more they are together and the more they do together, the happier, healthier, wealthier, wiser, and safer they all will live. The day when those words are frequently heard from the lips of humans all over that planet, those are the times when humans are putting huge distance between themselves and primitive cultures. Those are the days that truly belong to a more intelligent human species, the days that their ancestors dream of and prayed for, the times where humans' intelligence is too advanced to arm one another or separate their species by language or land mass.

Humans now have the knowledge to know all things are relevant and are taken into consideration, contributing to a more perfect union. Humans now utilizes advanced knowledge and advanced technologies that allow giant leaps forward in the state of the human conditions and the quality of the people's life spans on that planet. It's the highly intelligent behaviors that is nothing short of honoring themselves and their natural mother earth, so now their days and nights are all more meaningful and fulfilling, stress-free, happy, safe, and prosperous. The human species are now dwelling in a natural circle closer to themselves and to the creator "GOD," the host of all life forms on that magnificent planet they call Earth. That is where they all will be at their best "warm sweet spot."

Now they are qualified, able, and willing to manufacture and build much more suitable modern infrastructure to support better living conditions for all eight billion human lives. Now they have the proper ability to implement and enforce real, firm, true, and natural laws. Those discoveries of enhanced factual self-awareness and consensus produce the order that makes it easier to operate together as one family unit of human species. The type of order that is raising and nurturing the greatest human civilization, that as ever been seeing or experience by humans before. Finally, they are approaching the greatest existence they have ever known. Humans are finally approaching a type-one civilization intelligence as that planet faithfully hold its perfect position in a near timeless dance at the unimaginable speeds of about 67,000 miles per hour, revolving around "Sir Sun," her greatest star, the only star she has ever known. Their relationship is incredibly unique and special—a faithful and true partnership destined for life, all the life she finds herself cradling.

"They will never miss the waters until lakes go dry." Humans find themselves in a unique, special, and capable time in their life span. They are finally recognizing the true significance and importance of their existence. They are living on an incredible planet with no parameters on what they can accomplish for the good of all dwelling there as they find themselves currently being carried, cradled, and protected by the most magnificent beauty of a planet, their mother Earth, the only one of its kind that has ever been seen for millions of light years in and around this or other galaxies.

The human species is very special and unique, a magnificent creation, a prodigy given as a one-of-a-kind gift on a one-of-a-kind planet—sophisticated, intelligent, courageous, and durable both physically and mentally—yet in all their glory, the human babies are not born with an instruction manual. Instead, their human mind is firmly imprinted with the ability to mine "Truth"—the only manual they will ever need to lead an optimum quality life. The truth is the only operation manual the human species will ever need to properly coexist in a united operation of their life on that planet, navigating their mind and body to the best their planet has in store for each of them.

Truth is the ultimate guidance for all the life forms on planet Earth. The truth about planet Earth will always be firmly standing strong forever in time and space. The human species constantly try, but humans can never bring the truth to their term, but "Humans Must Come to Term with the Truth." The truth is the metaphorical pitstops that gets humans well-tuned to travel the generational road of life, free from disastrous outcomes, going through the right ways lit with greater understanding of the facts of life. Constant and forever, the truth will be their light, continuing to comfort, guide, and protect humans from dwelling amid darkness, lies, deception, or any harmful dangerous behaviors that disrespect the sacred sanctity of their life.

Following the misguidance of ignorance is moving away from the valuable knowledge humans need—the knowhow which will pave the way to the best conditions on earth, having the most meaningful and valuable commodities being available in more abundance to all humans including the rest of the species inhabiting their mother planet Earth. The time that brings all things to all life form has finally brought humans the eye-opening intelligence to see all the obstacles that are in their way, the disrespectful tricks that's stopping them from reaching the promised land of heavenly conditions. Most humans, as always, imagine heaven as a place far away, but now humans are awake with a better view, taking a closer look at the wisdom of themselves, realizing the true history of their primitive use of time, the proper understanding of their planet and her true history.

It's now general knowledge that heaven is right there on their planet Earth. Their knowledge increases tenfold and gives them the ears to hear and the eyes to see heavenly conditions. Wisdom grants the discernment to interpret the prophecy of heaven.

"Heaven is right above the earth, at human adult eye level, so the human children look up to heaven, but the human adults are face to face with heaven." Adults must teach the children how to find the truth in the best ways to inhabit their faithful mother planet. Human adults are responsible for their children's offenses until they reach age twelve. After age twelve, the children are responsible for their own choices to partake or resist the forbidden fruits in their own life span. If the parents of that generation are facilitating and utilizing advanced intelligence, then future generations will be enjoying an ever more intelligent way of life. Charting the best paths to live out their life spans on their home planet. Teach, mold, and straighten the children to come to the truth, which will always drive the future of humans into better living arrangement and conditions, nurturing the foundations of available heavenly conditions.

Understanding "heaven" is properly interpreting the truth. The word *heaven* is a metaphoric analogy of a living condition, not necessarily a place out there in the universe somewhere. Armed with that intelligence is the truth that will change the way humans live on their planet. Now they are relentlessly pursuing the reality of all the numerous possibilities to adequately and efficiently dwell on their beloved planet. They finally decided in one synchronized voice and one synchronized movement to seek out better living conditions courtesy of a new system instead of seeking out a new dwelling planet.

The human species has finally come of age, advancing further in the truth. The truth brings more good things to light. With the key to truth the purest, wisdom, knowledge, and technologies are unlocked. Now that they know how, they started to teach this intelligence to every human from the youngest to the oldest. Now this knowledge is common; the consensus is clear. Heaven is better living conditions that they all can live now right there on their planet. All the humans alive agree to that synchronized effort. They all took the sacred oath that they will always "do unto other humans as they would like other humans to do for them." Humans all acknowledge the more intelligent way to live is to show huge favors and love their neighbor the way they love themselves. With that sacred commitment to themselves and one another, the human species discovered the strongest building blocks to build a new system.

A valuable godly, intelligent alternative to the primitive and abusive money system, they now know the best way to guarantee all people everywhere on their planet a better quality of life—a higher standard of living that's safer and more pleasing to all eight billion of their life spans. After a vote on hundreds of potential systems from all sections of that planet, they all choose the easiest, fairest, most productive system—the superintelligence system that is not just favorable to a few but a highly advanced system that secure the best interests of all that is born to that planet.

"THE 449 UNITED UNION SYSTEM"—that's the one system they all felt was the best one to set the metaphoric dinner table for all eight billion of them, the first system of its kind, the only system in all human history with the super-intelligent means and generosity to guarantee every man, woman, and child absolute dignity and respect, with a comfortable seat at the metaphoric table of life, with new and advanced funding technology—a system that will give greater value to all people's life spans with the truth of this new system taught to the people. They are now willing to stand up firm and support a new system that adds way more value to their lives. They are lending the full support of their heart, mind, body, and time.

Humans all over that planet rejoice and sing the praises of the four-hour union system—four hours per day, four days per week, nine months per year. With that simple, easily manageable labor time schedule, human civilization rises to the dawn of a new day and time. Humans are now using time instead of outdated money for compensation for everything they utilize on earth. Time is the natural, pure, and true currency given to all humans by their creator GOD. They studied carefully the truth and effectiveness of the new system. With this new choice available now, 100 percent of the human population would never trade the new four-hour system backed by advanced digital funding technology and the massive four-hour worldwide union to go back to the primitive money use of time that's very disrespectful and degrading to the true value of human life, working people too hard and too long under the past tiresome premature system of ten to twelve hours per day, five to seven days per week, eleven to twelve months per year labor schedule.

Humans in every section of that planet, with the help of better, more intelligent leadership started synchronizing all labor on that planet into one huge four-hour labor union based on the facts that together they stand stronger and more efficient, divided they are inefficient and inadequate. That awareness encourages humans into sharing the labor burden for each man. Time brought them a true gift, which will keep on giving for the life of many, many generations—the knowledge and philosophy that more hands make work lighter and easier for the individual human participants in the four-hour labor force.

The human species in a united and synchronized effort finally got rid of their worst offender—the abusive inadequate money system that for thousands of years deceived and robbed them and their generations of the true fruits of their labors, disrespecting the true value of their sacred life and suppressing their peaceful freedoms, blocking the whole species of humans of a better, more advanced quality of life—the free lives they were all promised by the truth. They have finally found something that performs better and more valuable than money—the new improved advanced digital point system, "DPS," backed by the worldwide four-hour labor union. These two ambitious ideas combine to form one huge humanitarian friendly system.

Humans in every single corner of that planet are now on track to living their best life courtesy of the brand-new digital currency "DPS" supported by the easy and light four-hour-a-day labor union—finally the greatest breakthrough in human civilization. They do not need money anymore; they've found something new—a union with a brand new, more advanced digital currency that is a billion times more valuable to them than money. They found one another's corporation—the corporation that is accompanied by guarantees. This four-hour union system guarantees over one billion digital points for every single human child born on planet Earth backed by the most advanced, synchronized, people-friendly workforce ever developed by any human generation before on that planet, showing the more they are together and the more they work together in a synchronized four-hour worldwide labor force, the more valuable their time will be and the easier their life will be, making each of them wealthy, respected members for all their life span on that sacred planet with the strongest ever, well capable labor force of males and robots professionally trained and ready to carry the torch starting age twenty to the young retirement age of fifty with full benefits for life.

One of the best benefits of the DPS is females do not have to participate in the labor force while still enjoying full financial benefits for their life span due to the generosity of advanced, intelligent, and true real men. Turns out when the human's leadership synchronized all labor time into four-hour slots on all continents of that planet, there are more than enough able-bodied males out of eight billion humans ready to perform every job with the best quality—accurate and timely—with the help of next-generation robot technology capable of preproducing all the goods and services needed daily to support eight billion humans as one family. They were all enlightened that goods and services are best without the use of any money, a forbidden fruit to all humans.

The new DPS four-hour union significantly lightened the labor load and greatly improved the benefits for all people by employing a light and easy four-hour union system. This system conditions all labor time into four hours per day, four days per week, nine months per year sessions. These four-hour labor sessions by robots and able-bodied men eliminate the people's cost of living. This new funding of everything used time as their true natural currency, as proven, 2,000 percent more effective than money.

This new system of a synchronized labor force only need participation of able-bodied men aged twenty to fifty years old coupled with the help of work-capable robots programed and always ready to work, serving the best interest of a whole planet of humans while everyone enjoys the truth fruits of real freedom the way humans were meant to spend time on a planet. All humans are happy and proud of their new extended family of an advanced intelligent human species. As they all go about their days, spending precious time with one another, they're not spending time in a primitive struggle with money.

Humans are transferring from unsatisfying times to satisfied times—times when people spend no time primitively chasing money, which is now effectively known as the forbidden fruit. They are all now spending time reaping full benefit from their investment in the advanced super-intelligent new four-hour union system. Now people of all ages are spending more time relaxing and enjoying complete and free lifetimes, no more money chasing, no more living times poisoned by that forbidden fruit. Humans on their planet are all doing what they like to do best if it is lawful and not awful or harmful to their fellow humans. The human species is now "all aboard" the metaphoric financial system train, which have seated everyone and goes everywhere and passes through all continents on their planet, bringing good news and good tidings of better living conditions to all humans as they are carefully cradled on their mother planet Earth, traveling 76,000 miles per hour through time and space.

Humans are all feeling blessed by greater knowledge. They all are now living the true meaning of life by joining forces to intelligently serve one another's needs. Time has brought them good, refreshing knowledge backed by the latest technologies. The truth revealed through wisdom is sweeter that everything they have ever known. They were given more intelligent eyes to see life clearer. Their creator GOD already gave every human a free life and a free planet with an abundance of time, the only currency they will ever need for everything in a life span to enjoy living a wonderful life on their planet.

The true natural currency that is given to all humans is "TIME." Humans discovered a new formula that will metaphorically split the Adams of time into doing powerful, amazing, and greater things for the human species. Humans can now use time to pay for all goods and services with the touch of their finger instead of money. Truth gives knowledge, coupled with the latest technology, to build funding infrastructures in super systems based on four-hour labor time, not on money.

The money financial system that human suffered with for thousands of years has now ended. The truth lifts them up higher in understanding, so they can see further into the reality of a type-one civilization. They saw how counterproductive and even foolish it was to spend time employing a financial system that has 0 percent chance at a comfortable all-inclusive future. They saw future civilization without systems that's constantly deceiving them into false hope and forces them to work harder and longer as money slaves. They saw that they were working way too hard and too long of hours chasing money with very little results or satisfaction.

Time blesses them with the knowledge to see and to know that instead of being employed by a broken and abusive money system, greater knowledge gives them the eyes to see that money constantly degrade the value of human's worth. The money system is unsustainable to the future of humanity. They can now employ a new system that is fully sustainable, a funding system that will grant financial security to the human generation in a peaceful, comfortable, and total safe condition to all humans now and their future generations. They realize time is on loan from the creator, the free birth rights of all humans, a gift that should not be bought or sold. The human species acknowledge that they all must come to terms with that sacred truth and honor that fact. They were informed of and thought the truth that whatever they used to buy and sell, their most precious commodity of time was destined to become their biggest obstacle, the primitive deception of the abusive money system, which tricks and robs people out of years of good prosperous times.

Money became the middleman who robbed several generations of humans of the real fruits of their labor. The wisest ones warned human leadership not to buy and sell in their temple, which is their own body, mind, and soul. The truth reminded humans that "they all are sacred beings," a sacred life form that is given all things on that planet at no money cost. The only request was "to honor the truth and live by truth" in the spirit of true love. Disobeying those facts lead to humans wondering the fruited plains of that planet Earth in ruins, misery, and pain, abused and robbed, living in a broken, failed financial system based on buying and selling with the forbidden fruits of money what was given for free to all humans as a welcome gift to that planet.

All the materials for all goods and services on that entire planet was never for sale. They now see the reality that it is better to use the truth of humanity to build and employ a better funding system, better equipped to protect and serve all eight billion in the human species. Instead of trying to serve a primitive system based on primitive thinking primitively designed to serve selfishness and greed, such social economic designs are destructive to human living conditions and prosperous development.

Humans are very social beings that function best and thrive when their economic system is designed with all the parts equipped to serve all eight billion of them abundantly and easily. Anything less is counterproductive to their true values. With the greater intelligence of the truth, their minds rise above those misguided ways of living led by misguided leadership. They now know that if they are not living in the guiding lights of truth, they could become susceptible to the most misleading darkest of systems—the type of system that only promotes selfishness, greed, disappointments, and suffering. The type of living arrangements that produces no satisfaction for the humans involved, continuing to hopelessly lend support and dedication to a system that tricks them with money. Their new reality brought by time gave them new guidance to get past failed systems of inefficiency, replaced with a 7,000 percent more efficient four-hour system. They all are living the testimonies of true confessions.

> Man shall not live by bread alone, but by the ways of god's greater knowledge, the truly greatest intelligence for mankind. That meets the highest moral standards, and principles, molded in truth, and right.

They know now time brought them the knowledge to discern, the ears to hear, the eyes to see the truth. GOD is watching every single human separately and together as one species like a lifetime surveillance video camera—every day, every second, of all times—the sacred time and space given to every offspring of the human family, a most beloved species of life on a very special planet. In their lessons of life, they understand that the truth will always punish misbehaviors and reward good intelligent behaviors. It's now common lifesaving intelligence—"Humans can't run, leave their shadows, and they can't hide from the truth and time." They comprehend that all behaviors cause a ripple effect for everyone on that planet.

It has been discovered that for every action, there is an equal and opposite reaction. All things and behaviors are all relevant to everything on that planet. This knowledge causes humans to interact more intelligently with their fellow man. Time brought their intelligence up high enough; now they look out and see realizations of superintelligence, all premium times, in human civilization that prompt them to acknowledge instead of printing on primitive fabrics "IN GOD WE TRUST." It's much more productive and beneficial to live their sacred lives, trusting in the artful way of the truth that acknowledge reverence to truth, prompt the human population to begin building a brand-new well-needed united economic system.

Superintelligence gives them the new and advanced "DPS four-hour labor union." They realize that they have outgrown the old economic system based on money, buying and selling goods, and time. Humans all know now that buying and selling all that was given freely to the species is a very destructive behavior which should never be repeated—the digital point system, "DPS," backed by a worldwide four-hour labor union, a united union that's designed to take the best care of all humans from before birth up to the grave, e volving to take full advantage of the vast, incredible powers of numbers.

Mathematics, correctly fused with time, will provide all the needs of countless human generations for millions of years to come. Numbers never lie, and time is a plentiful gift on loan from GOD. Humans can now see that when they couple time with their numbers, give them the power and resources they need to reach and uplift the living conditions of all eight billion humans on that planet by establishing a union of one united work force for their planet, a union that only requires payment at the fair price of time served, only four hours per day, four days per week, nine month per year for only thirty years, from only able-bodied man and work function robots.

This time served in the DPS four-hour union by just able-bodied males and highly intelligent robots programmed to the needs of the people satisfies all debts by eliminating the cost of living for all humans born to that magnificent super planet Earth, finally intelligently mature enough to answer the desperate emergency call of the people to higher quality living conditions, the most intelligent way to spend humans' life spans using time modified mathematics coupled with their huge numbers of people. The new system stays constantly, efficiently, resourcefully supplying all the goods and services to the needs of all in the human species for their life span. This economic powerhouse pays out all humans for life. This remarkable turbo of a four-hour system is so well designed, built strong, firm, and solid—enough to only require participation from males aged twenty to age fifty. When they run the numbers, it reflects a labor force that is strong and robust, with numbers hovering at about 2.5 billion able-bodied men per year coupled with the work force of about 3.5 billion robots programed to work anywhere anytime, constantly passing the labor torch to new members, replacing the retirees with new members every day.

Humans all love this advanced new economic system, "DPS," united four-hour union because they all spend less time at work and have more free time to spend doing what they like best. They are pleased with the greater value added to their life span based on synchronized scheduled four-hours-a-day time slots. They all step away from the slave labor times of the primitive throwback money. The females, children, and elderly all praise this system. Their group participation in the labor union is not necessary.

There are over five billion healthy male hands and countless high-tech machinery and robots that make all work light—in fact so light only a fraction of the human population is needed to carry the workload, volunteering men performing their civic duties of four-hour days for four days a week between the age of twenty to fifty. Everyone else is free to enjoy the fruits of intelligent synchronized labor coupled with the latest technology in robotics. Time evolves them, the everlasting gift, which has plenty to give—a long-awaited revolutionary support management, a brilliant synchronization of all labor time. They took a giant leap forward in the ability to organize and build the greatest uninterrupted distribution system, presupplying all goods and services to all that has life on their planet, delivering true independence with a synchronized force of men and robots, relentless in attending all the needs of every life born to their time on their miraculous planet. All the women, children, and elders enjoy real freedom and creature comforts as they all pass time, hopping the map of geographical locations on their mother earth.

Time showed humans that the type of social economic system they need for the best quality living conditions works better with bigger, stronger, healthier participation numbers. Based on that fact, they started preserving their numbers with greater values. Humans abruptly stop killing one another first and then immediately cease from killing human babies by abortions. They are now blessed with the wisdom of knowing the more they do together, the easier, more comfortable life becomes. They now realize they need all the babies they can produce to keep the life of this system going strong and healthy. Humans now in tune with the ways of the truth know the sure signs of a healthy human society—is when the born living humans are preparing physically, mentally, and emotionally to receive all unborn humans with a valuable system ready to welcome every single unborn into important positions to become a valuable new member of a highly intelligent generation that teaches their minds the important morals and values of returning the same favor to the next generation of unborn humans.

Now that well-oiled machine of synchronized labor powers the engine of the metaphoric train, bringing the good tidings of real true help, financial security that produce an environment of joyful peace in all corners of their ever faithful, generous, and kind mother planet. This new digital technology takes full advantage of the ability to share everything generously to all life on that planet. Now humans are discovering true and proper knowledge for addressing all obstacle to optimum quality life span. Slowly but surely, time brings better, more advanced condition, sufficiently prearranging all goods and services each day. Humans are relieved and grateful that they've found something new and better than money. They all can see now that money over time constantly loses its value. That primitive idea was never able to pay for everything their species needs for easy living such as a more comfortable, meaningful quality of life. Money was not able to pay for educating their young with the proper teachers-to-students ratios.

While the DPS united four-hour union provides one teacher to every ten students ratio all the time in all the schools, the money could not pay for all their protection. The DPS four-hour union security branch makes it top priority to ensure the safety of all humans on the planet, virtually eliminating human violence on their planet. It doesn't matter where on that planet they happen to be; their safety is always guaranteed—it's top priority. The DPS four-hour system gives new meaning to the phrase "safety is number 1 priority." The humanitarian protection force guarantees everyone safe living conditions as they move about their planet even though crime is virtually nonexistent. They accomplish remarkable safety records by establishing a ratio of ten safety officers to every one hundred humans everywhere on that planet all the time.

In truth, they uncover there is knowledge for that type of individual security and protection for all humans, where every human has the options of body cams with quick-response alarms, the type that pay attention to details, personal and universal protection that money couldn't buy. Their medical system is now 1,000 percent more advanced and efficient. Now all humans get immediate medical attention on demand twenty-four-seven, 365 days per year at no charge everywhere on the entire planet courtesy of the vast network of doctors provided by the people's DPS four-hour union whatever location in the planet they may need it, always maintaining a brilliant and dedicated doctors-to-patients ratio.

The DPS union medical wing takes on the enormous and complicated task of providing immediate medical attention to all those who need it with no money involved. They synchronize this humongous task by strategically placing state-of-the-art medical facilities at the ratio of one facility per every three thousand humans. Money could never be enough to pay for such complex, sophisticated, and dedicated medical system for all. The species rejoice and give thanks for their blessing of a new always advancing medical system. Humans used the latest tech and add the best part of all—they made all medical services easily accessible and readily available to all people and all other life forms on that planet with only a mere finger touchscreen at points of service with the state of their medical system intelligently efficient.

Human decided to take on travel with the understanding that their early ancestor was nomad. It's human nature to want to travel constantly. With that understanding of their true nature, the new DPS system, a united synchronized four-hour labor force, decided to make it very easy for humans to travel from point A to B anywhere on that planet they are to anywhere on the planet they wish to go. This massive undertaking is a huge task, but humans have been ready to remove all the obstruction that keep them from traveling to all the destination that they seek on their planet home, first started by building millions of modern roads and train tracks crisscrossing all the landmasses on the entire planet, accompanied by new-generation semiautonomous vehicles with the options of manual or self-driving modes. They build thousands of state-of-the-art airports strategically placed according to populations dotting their planet all over.

To support the brand-new fleet of superintelligent, durable flying machines ever seen before on that planet, with the best safety record second to none seen before. For boats, ferries, and ships, humans build huge numbers of easily accessible ports and docks with a new advanced fleet of virtually unsinkable boats and ships making it safer and more efficient to move about for all water travelers everywhere with the campaign to make traveling safer, easier, more efficient for all in the human species on that planet now so successful. They remove the final obstacle by eliminating the need for any passport to travel from one section of the planet to another section of their planet. All humans need now in this blessed time to travel is a simple finger touch of a screen at points of service.

The "DPS" united four-hour union put a new transportation system in place, and they cover all the stops, making travel simple and easy at no individual cost. Humans all find it so refreshing and convenient that they don't need primitive money to travel anymore. They are all supported by the endless metaphoric pockets of the DPS united four-hour labor union. They are all amazed by the difference digital points make in their day-to-day life as opposed to using the throwback thief money. Money is the idea of primitive time spent wasting people precious life span. Now that humans all over that planet are enjoying the full fruits of their labor, they almost can't believe the full access they have to all goods and services in abundance. They're all pleased and thankful for the time that bring them life more abundantly. Humans are now sticking to the truth and nothing but the truth, so help them "GOD." Their possibility is endless.

Now that they all realize the fact that out of many,they're all "ONE" family of one human species. It didn't matter what section of the once separated planet they originate from. It didn't matter what shade was their natural skin color, and it certainly didn't matter which one of the many separating languages they used. Time brings them the light to see now and for all their life spans. They're truly members of one planetwide family unit.

Once the truth reveal itself, humans everywhere all join in a synchronized relentless pursuit to remove all the ignorance that present any obstacle from their giant family reunion. They all agree speaking different languages on that planet is counterproductive to the ambitious goals of a more perfect union—the highly advanced, super-intelligent, sacredly connected human civilization which is the true home of humanity. So they set out on the very ambitious task of teaching one language to all the human species on that planet. They made what was once difficult now made easy. They fight against the language barrier until it doesn't exist anymore between planet residents.

The removal of that obstacle did wonders to improve their ability to join forces in efficiently accessing the goods and services for all human's daily consumption on that planet, starting with first getting an accurate count of every single man, woman, and child on every square foot of that planet. Then they all join forces through the huge four-hour labor union to take on the enormous task of prearranging, designing, manufacturing, producing, and delivering all the goods and services every human will ever need for their well-funded time frames of life from cradle to grave.

When humans now look back and see all the paradise living that was being robbed from their existence by the money's disease system, they now rejoice for their peace and safety, their caring and sharing, their incredible ability to synchronize and share all labor time to make work as easy as four hours a day to support a family. In consideration of their true nomad ways, humans can now keep a four-hour work schedule anywhere on the planet they may choose to live or work. Such freedom and versatility could never be accomplished by the primitive, abusive, outdated times of money.

The whole species of humans are now living in amazing, modified time. They all wonder why time didn't bring them the knowledge of this new improved and complete system sooner, but they spend no time looking backward. They are here now, and they have everything they need—the full and unwavering cooperation of one another. They can see now where they went wrong. They all realize the knowledge of true help was always patiently awaiting their arrival in time all the time. Even though nothing is done before it's time, it's best not to be caught behind time.

Time is the greatest force humans and all they can interact with will ever know. Time is the source that gives and takes all. Now the human species are coming of age from their adolescent ignorant time. The inadequate, immature, misguided, destructive behaviors that's responsible for so much wicked, evil atrocities against humans in past times. God, the truth, forgives them all. They didn't know the seriousness of their destructive behavior that's responsible for the pain and hurt they caused one another. They all come to realize that time is on their side—literally in their pockets because God gave every single human an abundance of time as currency for the road trip of life. Any other currency is like a deadly disease, an obstacle in their way to unification on that planet. Armed with the facts of planet life, they all teach and studied the wisdom that gave them this knowledge—the knowledge that realizes the technology that digitally points all humans in the right, true direction, the direction that moves the people's intelligence forward in the mode of doing everything with the best intelligence, efficient and advanced, according to truth.

Like a billboard in their minds, they all can see that "GOD'S KNOWLEDGE IS GREATER" to give all humans the best conditions of intelligent life. The species discover there's different dimensions of time on their beautiful planet. They realize that they can occupy time amid darkness, which would bring forth abuse and suffering, or they can occupy time in the circle of the lighted truth, which guarantees shared prosperity through true love.

God speaks through the truth, and the truth leads humans to good knowledges which in turn produces intelligence that will build and utilize advanced new technology—the type of technology that modified time into the comfort zone of heavenly conditions accommodating all life on their planet, each playing their own solid positions in their rights to live life in ever-satisfying modes, indulging in time frames modified to living life more abundantly now and for all their future generations.

There's so much time available for the human species to live in the proper living conditions—happily living in paradise, inhabiting mansions, courtesy of their intelligent behaviors toward one another. Truly no man, woman, or child left behind, funded by the long-awaited four-hour financial system that covers all the bases. The four-hour united labor union applied correctly with the truth is real-life assistance to one and all humans. Humans tried in past time to employ other false, unfaithful assistance from corrupt ruled systems but failed miserably. Humans now know there's a supreme order and firm rules to their planet seen and unseen working with the facts of their lives. They can comprehend that if one of them push a boulder off the top of a hill, it will roll down to the lowest point, "it's gravity."

When they invented a system that buy and sell what was given to them in abundance free, it's the heights of arrogance and ignorance lacking integrity. Building, and employing a system that serves all of humanity adequately require true integrity from all members of a generation. The new digital point system makes it easy for all humans to be true and kind to themselves and one another. All humans have a very important role to play as a part of the four-hour union system. With true integrity, they all go about their days with one another's best interest at heart. Now the members of the human species completely understand. That's the premium way life was truly meant to be lived on their planet, loving and sharing in abundance all things that was given to them as planet gifts.

The "DPS" is not a physical currency. That means it cannot be stolen or duplicated. Humans cannot hoard or mind these points. In fact, the DPS is endless funding for human life span accessible by touch screen at all points of service for the sole purpose of keeping track of inventory and services rendered because the DPS is a brand-new never-seen-in-use-before digital point system. Used as natural currency, it can never be insufficient funds for the over eight billion humans on that planet enjoying the unwavering access to the system with enough points daily. Easily accessible to every individual by fingerprint touch screen, it's truly priceless.

This idea is so much more advanced, sufficient, and efficient for the ever-growing needs of humanity. They are way past the times when humans used to back money by gold only to abandon that idea. When they slowly realized there was not enough gold for the huge amount of money, they will need to support the ever-expanding needs of generations of humans. However, they continue to print on fabric in attempt to control the value of human labor and their planet's free goods only to be metaphorically hit head on with the truth.

Money is the root of all evil, clearly a forbidden fruit. The days when humans strayed from the truth and decided to invent an unnatural currency and call it money, this idea caused massive damage to human relations. That action caused many negative reactions, inducing unrighteous behaviors that produces and facilitate greed, selfishness, dishonesty, desperation, robbery, and all manner of unpleasant characteristics and behaviors, wreaking havoc among the human population on that planet.

Humans' general knowledge is now elevated to be more adequate for their planet life span journey. New intelligence has all eyes wide open; they can see clearly now. The greed in the money system continues to raise the price of everything—all the valuable resources they need for an easy, comfortable, high quality of life in a very short average eighty years for people. The cost of everything kept going up higher and higher in turn, making them work harder and longer for their daily needs.

Humans realize there is no hope in money in a futuristic type-one human civilization. It's a system that degrades, controls, and limits the value of their work and worth. It's a diseased system that's responsible for the corrosion of human behavior toward their immediate and extended family members, continuing to bring human society further and further down into the abyss of human's worse characteristic and behaviors—all while fueling greed, selfishness, envy, jealousy, hate, dishonesty, deception, mayhem, and murder. Money is the root that springs out into all these negative behaviors in humans.

From false ideas and lies, humans build a system that they could not control, a system that turned and took control of their lives, turned them into slaves, to money, a rootless master—a master that they were all forced to worship, a master that with no mercy brutalized many generations of humans in countless ways over an enormous length of time until time brought them greater knowledge—God's true greater knowledge. Now they're all free to build systems that doesn't work with the diseased money or for the primitive ways of money. Now the entire human species, instead, works on building the DPS united four-hour union based on the true value of the individual human natural currency of time.

Time is the natural currency on loan to humans from God. Anything else the human species try to replace that natural currency with is destined to corrupt and fail them miserably. Now the human species are training their minds into understanding, accepting, and acknowledging the facts of their life spans on the fruitful planes of that planet.

Time on loan from God should never be for sale by any human anywhere. Time came to humans and show them the true figures of a complete life. They finally figured out life is a puzzle that must be put together properly, or else, they will all suffer the grave consequence of the lack of this knowledge. Humans should not live by food alone, but they must adopt the right and true principles, morals, and values closest to GOD, the rules and guidance of purified laws that revolve around the best interests of all the majestic generations of humanity.

Disobeying these guidance leads humans into endless wars, committing heinous atrocities against one another, harboring the evils of the darkest times of human lives, embracing the ignorance that holds them, wasting precious time and countless lives—a grave sacrifice to the lack of knowledge of better ways, the ways to incorporate their real identity of caring and sharing everything through love for one another.

The highly advanced specialized DPS four-hour united labor union has the integrity needed to incorporate all those natural traits into positive and lucrative actions for goodwill toward all of humanity. The DPS union came just in time to save humanity from the constant suffering of their generations. There is great knowledge for human unification hovering that planet, and time finally brought relief and comfort gift wrapped to their generations now. The human species is now aware that they can easily spend time instead of money for all necessities on that planet. It's God's manner to acquire the knowledge that condition time into enough goods and services for every human need with endless extras.

The God-given knowledge of the amazing digital point system found the ability to turn love into very real lucrative goods and services—literally coming to the aid of every human that is born in this time frame. Humans now found the way to pay for the equivalence of trillions of dollars' worth of goods and services every day—from just four hours' labor time slots synchronized into a global four-hour union workforce to intelligently direct the new globally synchronized four-hour united union labor force. They join themselves in a huge number of men ages twenty to fifty filling every four-hour time slot for all official labor. The human's species was and is never short of anything. Having everything good, generously is the way the truth of GOD meant human life to inhabit that planet. Everything there was always free for all the members of the human's species and all lifeform on that planet. Nothing was ever for sale until misguided humans invented money.

Money was the devil's way to stay relevant in God's human species. Money was the inherent middleman that robbed upwards of 90 percent of human free time, labor, and worth. Money is the forbidden fruit of advanced human civilization. Money is like the disease, and this new four-hour system is like the cure. Now with that catastrophe passed, humans are now free to live life in the circle of the truth, closer to GOD where they all were ordained to live.

Bringing a four-hour global labor union fully operational was not an easy task. There was a lot of skepticism and pushback from those humans who did not yet see that light, but the truth of humanity must be revealed to its rightful generations. So, the good news of the new system spread fast to all humans in this time frame. The time has come to the generation of this time frame to enjoy the riches of a global digital point system. They've finally recognized something more valuable than money and gold—the times that modified their lifestyle for better days. The whole human species on that planet was ready and anxious for its implementation. Humans all decided to take a planetwide yeah or nay vote. The old money system did not stand a chance.

Overwhelmingly, the human species voted 97 percent (yeah!) to 3 percent (nay!) to move into a new system of spending time instead of money for the livelihood of their generation's life span. They all decided to give this new system a reality test. Humans decided to test this new "DPS" four-hour labor system on one of the planet's many small islands. They put a call out to one hundred thousand volunteers. They all decided to test this system for ten years to see how well it will perform in real time. So, they start choosing one hundred thousand humans from different age groups from all over that planet.

In order to ensure true, real results, all in the human population had to be reflected. One hundred thousand humans were chosen from five different age groups. They chose twenty thousand humans ages five to fifteen, twenty thousand ages sixteen to twenty-five, twenty thousand ages twenty-six to thirty-five, twenty thousand ages thirty-six to forty-five, twenty thousand ages forty-six to fifty-five years old. No one was surprised; there was no shortage of volunteers. Everyone all over the planet lined up to try the new system of all-in-one better living conditions, but it was only a trial run; everyone couldn't participate yet. They had to be specific in which humans they choose for the huge test of a different type of funding system. They had to choose humans familiar or trained in the necessary roles they needed to play in the correct ratio to the one hundred thousand number of them joining the test run.

They got started by choosing doctors or humans trained in the medical field. For a ratio of five humans medically trained for every one hundred people, they chose officers or humans trained in conflict resolution at a ratio of five peace officers for every one hundred people. They chose judges to uphold the true integrity of a law-and-order human society at a ratio of one judge for every three thousand participants. They chose farmers or humans trained in agriculture at a ratio of ten farmers for every on thousand participants. They chose mechanics or humans trained in manufacturing and maintaining machineries and engines at the proper ratio of equipment needed. They chose computer tech engineers responsible for manufacturing and maintaining all computers and robotic technology according to proper needs. They chose electricians to manufacture and maintain all electrical needs accordingly. They chose teachers or humans with educator background according to proper ratio needs. They chose carpenters or humans with building background. They chose plumbers and those with water maintenance knowledge. They chose professional and assistance in all the many jobs needed to be done in a modern human civilization. They chose everyone according to the proper service ability to the ratio of the one hundred thousand of them needed for that very important ten years test run.

After everyone was chosen, all one hundred thousand of them were transported to that island by airplanes in back-to-back flights scheduled fast to get everyone on the island quickly. After all participants were safely on that island, the first order of things was to pick a strong, qualified leader, so the call went out for humans with leadership experience. Twenty-five humans stepped forward, and out of twenty-five, five finalists were chosen. These five were each asked to write a two-page essay explaining what this experiment meant to them and what ideas they would use to enhance the best interest of all the participants. They were given twenty-four hours to come up with their own unique essay that reflect the best interest of all the people of that island.

After twenty-four hours passed, each was asked to read their essay on TV for everyone to see and hear. All five got their chance to read their essay; that was broadcasts to everyone on the island. All one hundred thousand humans watched, paying close attention knowing that once they see and heard all five humans read their essay, they would have to pick the one they felt reflected the best leadership intelligence.

Once all 5-leadership essay was broadcast, the participants have twenty-four hours to choose by electronic fingerprint voting from their cell phones. They chose the one that seemed to be more sincere and honest, the one that seemed to have the integrity qualified to be their leader. All the votes were tallied with no possibility of any fraud or miscalculation. All fingerprints were electronically verified and accounted for. They chose one of the five by a large margin of 71 percent of all the votes. He was the one that is going to lead his generation to take a giant leap forward in time, defying the gravity of their past situations and living conditions.

They timely set that leader in place and established the rules to live by. They implemented a few simple laws:

1. Humans must never arm another human.
2. Humans must never lie to or deceived another human.
3. Humans must always behave in the best interests of all.
4. Humans should love all other humans as they love themselves.
5. Humans must do unto all other humans as they would like other humans to do for them.

Those are the foundational laws that will govern the living conditions of all participants on the island. This was taught to all the humans in this test run. They all agreed and understood that this is a system, more of a self-government. This system works best when everyone understands, upholds, and lives by the principles of truth and rights. All one hundred thousand of them clearly know in their minds that humans should not live by food, clothes, and shelter alone but by the greatest truth of principles, morals, and values. Everyone acknowledges that they are all there to serve one another to achieve the best quality of life for all who are participating with true understanding of their purpose.

They all set out to have a wonderful cutting-edge of humanity lifestyle. The leader they chose assumed his duties and started appointing head leaders to all the supporting branches needed to properly guide one hundred thousand humans in an autonomous society on that island. He chose the head of all major branches needed to support all the participants properly.

The wise leader appointed four zones on the island with four managers of each zone—a move designed to make it easier to attend the needs of everyone more accurately. He appointed in all four zones the head of all medical facilities and services, the head of all law and order, the head of all roads and transportation, the head of all farming and food distribution, the head of all housing and building, the head of all utilities and water supplies.

With the leaders of all four zones in place, the massive undertaking began to manufacture and supply all goods and services needed for comfortable living conditions for every single human on that island. All one hundred thousand of them understood that this is a new system and everything will be done differently. There is no money in use, no biting the forbidden apple—that trick from the devil is deceased. They all agree to take giant leaps away from a money system that was causing tyranny for the majority and masquerading as help for a few, paving the way to the introduction of the new digital point system, "DPS," backed by all their corporations, sealed with a fingerprint-signed agreement.

They all confirm that their duties are to serve one another. Their goal is to live truth in philosophies that promote productive behavior toward one another. Their vision is to create the environment in a society where all understand the greater knowledge to "serve and share, so all will be served and receive their share." They promise to work together in a synchronized four-hour labor force, a unification four-hour union that pays the people's cost of living. A united four-hour labor union that will coordinate and synchronize all official labor on the island into four-hour time slots. That four-hour time slot is the official energy cube of time that powers everything on that island for everyone. This is an ingenious new way of sharing the labor burden into four-hour time slots—slots that only need to be filled by able-bodied men ages twenty to ages fifty coupled with advanced intelligent robots programmed to work anywhere at any time. They took a count of all able-bodied males within that age range. They came up with 30 percent of the one hundred thousand people; the other 70 percent were either too young, past fifty, or female.

Greater true knowledge understands and supports this united arrangement that's providing a comfortable, peaceful environment for the young, elders, and females to be free from the stress of any financial obligation to attend to their own natural daily needs without the added burden or pressure of any official labor. That is best for everyone in a healthy futuristic human civilization. They embrace the best knowledge on how to proceed forward without burdening or stressing any individual with more than they can bear.

All goods and all services are adequately provided to every human by the most advanced synchronized labor system any human civilization has ever enjoyed. This union made life so much easier and efficient. Humans in the work years age range only work four hours a day, four days a week, nine months out of a year to fulfill their obligation to the system. Once each human who is part of the workforce fulfilled their four-hour obligation of civic duties, they're then free to live in the best of times, just enjoying their life spans. This advanced type of planning brings out better-quality lifetimes—times when human behaviors will measure up at their best, when human modified time to be easier, safer, healthier, in more productive ways to live on planet Earth.

This system guarantees everyone all the goods and services they could ever need for life without the use of money, just the use of their time, because now humans have the knowledge and the tech to condition life spans arranged with the best times unlike the failed past social economic system. This new system doesn't ask humans for money; it only requires designated short amounts of their time to the DPS four-hour system union. This system works best when humans leave greed and gluttony behind. This system doesn't judge human wealth by how much things they possessed but by how much they are able to share of their time on loan from the creator. They all were informed that they can't really claim anything on that planet because it's all on a short average eighty-year loan from God. They all understood that certain behaviors are counterproductive to the goal of comfortably seating all people to the dinner table of life. They all join forces in a massive building and farming project.

They set out to build everything they will use and need, starting with building comfortable housing for all one hundred thousand of them, state of the art medical facilities. They employ the latest in farming technologies producing the best, most nutritional foods linked with the logistics of the most efficient distribution facilities with the option of home delivery. That means no going hungry or lack of anything for anyone. They design, manufacture, and build their own vehicles for all use—official and recreational. They design and construct the safest roads crisscrossing that island all according to the proper ratio of serving all one hundred thousand of them and their communities.

This is a self-serve autonomous island; they all manufactured and built everything themselves. They had everyone in place to build and maintain everything they need. They properly delegated all the services that will be needed. They began quickly training qualified participants to fill the 30 percent work force numbers they needed. They decided to quickly train and place men and robots in their four-hour slot. Once the four-hour union became alive, they started filling all the labor hours needed to take the best care of the upgrade island people. They started producing homes with the latest in creature comfort with smart tech electronics and appliances starting from comfortable one-family up to ten-family homes that are always available for all the families used.

All the housing are available as timeshare, accessible to everyone through digital points, touch screen. All vehicles for official, personal, or recreational use is available to everyone courtesy of a sophisticated efficient timeshare system of transportation, a transport system that guarantees by contract that every human would be transported to anywhere on the planet they wish to go by whatever means they wish to travel—land, air, or sea—it's the new law. They're all following the script of greater knowledge that showed leaders the satisfying benefit of having everything on that island available as preapproved timeshared. This type of availability makes living easier, more efficient, less burdensome for everyone, with the understanding based in the true nature nomad roots of humans. People rather just have the use of things as the need arise instead of being saddled with ownership and maintenance cost. They all rather live life in a time when humans are not tied to objects, wasting precious time to the tune of years of stress from payments, storing, maintenance, and all the foreseen issues of owning. They all just want the best of the two, which is always having access to all things as their daily needs require.

The DPS four-hour green union guarantees access to every object or anything any participant needs at that moment or as their needs change day to day. "Any object or any service is no object"— anything in the form of vehicles, houses, medical attention, foods, clothes—anything—or assistance they may need at any given moment in time are all guaranteed by contract. This incredible network of time sharing everything gives humans so much more free time and freedom to enjoy their short life span of planet life. No more wasting time babysitting things and objects.

With the money out of the way, humans are face to face with the facts. Humans and their well-being are always more important than anything or objects on that planet. They all face the truth that the objects they sometimes love more than people are made only to serve the needs of humans. Humans are given dominion over a planet; therefore, nothing on that planet is more valuable or more sacred than human life and the condition of people's life. Humans can now clearly see the lies of a money system that deceives and tricks many of them into holding objects higher than themselves and other human life. They all now highly anticipate living a new philosophy with heightened self-awareness that elevate their ways of thinking and living on that island. They all now are being taught a higher-intelligence awareness that leads them on the relentless pursuit of mining new knowledge—hidden knowledge that's constantly awaiting the people's discovery, the understanding that's teaming with advanced ways how to inhabit that planet in easy mode out of adolescence to the maturity of an advanced type-one civilization where humans all acknowledge the facts of a true planet love to live life in a love to live mode.

Always holding sacred human life is most important over everything on their planet with that elevated intelligence of who they are and their massive capabilities. They all seek God's greater knowledge, which gives easy access to all the enormous amounts of resources on their planet. Humans leap forward by building all things to serve their needs, assigning no values to things and objects the way the truth would have it. All the objects they build: houses, vehicles, equipment, robots, machinery, etc.—all things and objects one can imagine—were all built for the express purpose of serving the needs of humanity and enhancing the quality of human life.

There is no value added to any object. Humans now rely on intelligent logistics of manufacturing, reproducing, and delivering replacement of all objects by the united DPS four-hour union system as needed. This all-inclusive way of living is the new way of inhibiting a planet. It's the way to guarantee to every human that they will never be short of any supplies or service on that planet ever again. All one hundred thousand participants on that island were all on the good road to the cutting edge of the evolution of humanity. The wise leader of this very important test run of this revolutionary technologically advanced easy way of living decided to address the participants in this speech heard around the planet:

Good morning, afternoon, evening to all of you, my fellow humans God's magnificent creations. He said I bring good news and good tiding to y'all. There are the good times, a bright day in the journey of human evolution on our planet. Time has brought us here to the dawn of a new day and time—the times where humankind intelligence is elevated to new heights, that heights where humans will never want for anything on this planet ever again, the heights where we find true love in appropriate new words in communications. The right ways to hold our eight billion and growing members' family bonds stronger than ever, never to be broken again.

The enemies of our unity and well-being are singled out, surgically removed, and separated from us forever. Thanks to the discovery of our new sophisticated superior-quality type-one civilization intelligence that can now see and identify the enemy whenever it approaches the human circle. We will enforce the truth that will bless our sacred innovative lifestyle in our brand-new living conditions. The truth teaches humans only suffer from the lack of knowledge. Now that time has passed. We all now have that precious knowledge. God's greater knowledge always knows best for humans. Now humanity has finally found the way to utilize that knowledge for all to enjoy with the guidance of truth fused with God's greater knowledge, we're quickly approaching humanity's "promised land"—a time when new knowledge gives us all highly intelligent technology to work together easy and light, the time when more organized hands make life, living, work, and conditions much easier, lighter, and favorable for all.

From the humble beginning of our new system, we will implement massive helpful changes. We are going to advance love from just a word to pure incredible actions—the actions that are aided with the technologies that is relentlessly in the pursuit of always attending the needs of every human on this planet every second, minute, hour of each day now and for all human life span. We finally found what it takes to unleash the forever giving power of our creator's generous blessing. Superintelligence brought heaven, the living condition in the view of humans hovering at eye level where it always dwells awaiting the right, bright, and wise generation to utilize all and share all—the human generation that emerges from primitive times, with eyes wide open to seeing, knowing, and enjoying the living conditions that was promised to mankind by the truth.

The greater dimensions of the truth of our planet is no longer a hidden treasure. I say unto all of you within the sound of my humble voice, this generation is the one that is intelligent and mature enough for the rewards of our ancestors' hardship and prayers. Today is the day, and this is the time when the truth delivers to humans the gift that will keep on giving the innovative technology, which maps new living conditions on our planet, the intelligent living that exercises a pure type of love—the love which transforms and satisfies all humans as one family on this planet. The truth gives us these times in these bright days to take giant leaps away from the dying, corrupt, misleading political system and the outdated primitive abusive financial system.

We are going to combine our God-given most precious commodity of time into a truly unbreakable circle of a most sacred and solid bond, a commitment to the well-being of every human on our magnificent planet. This true commitment to our humanity is clearly our next reality by discarding the old failed primitive financial system and adopting the use of our natural currency of "time" modified to a digital points system, the most valuable commodity that is given to all humans free in abundance.

We are the first generation that is going to utilize this elevated intelligence to shape time into providing all we could ever need for our life span. The human life on this planet was meant to live worry-free with all things available in abundance. God's greater knowledge declared to the wisest generation—our generation—that nothing is to be for sale on this planet. A family that understands and practices true love in its purest forms knows that it is immoral, foolish, and counterproductive to buy or sell anything on planet Earth—buying or selling our precious, and priceless resources of goods and services to our own human family members. That practice by humans is the definition of eating of the forbidden fruits. That behavior is embracing a corrupt disease system.

Greater knowledge and greater times brought us the most intelligent cure. We must stop immediately buying or selling everything on this planet. It's all ours, a precious lifeline that is given to humans freely by our sacred creator of planet Earth. We humans are a magnificent work of art given to this planet as stewards of all things. We finally arrive here in the times to claim our rightful place and our rightful living conditions in the sacred domains of what is all our equal rights to a better-quality life on our planet.

With greater understanding, humans are farming new financial landscape, undersigned contracts with the entire human family for the first time in human history with the cooperation of all able-bodied male lending their most precious commodity of time in four-hours-a-day time slot for four days per week, nine months a year until they turn fifty years old. We will use this precious commodity of able-bodied men—time—with the help of robots in the most effective and sacred of ways to building the new system that is responsible for constantly attending the needs of every single human, always twenty-four hours a day, 365 days a year for their life span on our planet.

By paying all their bills with the new smart digital funding technology, one of the most valuable products, to propel our generation into a type-one civilization of superintelligence coded in truth's philosophical, metaphorical analogies, aided with the most advanced knowledge and technology, robots and machinery, we are going to send the loudest, clearest, most recognizable message to all destructive elements or criminal behavior that may consider development.

Our planet is a true law-and-order crime-free zone from this day forward. We will utilize the latest crime-fighting technology to surgically remove crime and destructive behavior from human existence. For any challenger who are nonbelievers, we will prove it. If any human so much as harm one hair on any other human's head, we, the people united "DPS" four-hour union collaborative planet security force, will find them, wheeling endless resources to eliminate crime that money could not pay for to bring them to the front of the congregation. The correction councilors will account for their action, which will be met with the appropriate corrections.

We are making a promise and commitment to always have peace officers available, to serve all the people in synchronized four-hour shifts, twenty-four hours a day, for the safety needs of all eight billion humans on our planet. This new system is a united effort to always guarantee the safety of every child, woman, and man residing on our planet. For the first time in human history, we will provide the environment where humans don't worry about their personal safety or fear arm from other humans on our planet anymore ever again. That is the new rule of human engagement planetwide that will be vigorously enforced. Anything less than a law-and-order human society is unacceptable. We are using God's greater knowledge to educate all humans on how to always properly and politely engage and interact with fellow humans.

As the most advanced generation, our commitment to one another is to educate every member of the human family with advanced knowledge for free with special attention to the young—our children are all our future—attending to our children with the absolute best care. Raising them in a healthy, safe environment is simultaneously attending to all our future in the most intelligent ways. The truth shows us that it is counterproductive and igno-rant to charge our own children for educa-tion. We will make it our top priority to teach the children how to become good stewards of humanity. We are going to educate all our chil-dren for free with the latest and most intelligent knowledge, preparing them to be ready to take the torch of prosperity, to continue to support future generations—from the unborn to all human's life spans—staying true to the proper, more advanced living conditions that we were all meant to live, happy, and enjoy a stress-free planet.

We are the generation that is blessed with the intelligence to master living conditions on our planet, in tune with all our senses. We will build a system that will utilize the best of human nature which in turn will produce the best of human behaviors. We will provide the environment suitable for cultivating love, the greatest bonding emotion human feels. God's greater knowledge gives this generation the intelligence to mine the power and dimensions of love using the purest, deepest love of human-ity to aid us in our most ambitious quest to live out the true meaning of our existence by serv-ing one another's needs from the unborn cradle to the grave.

We owe it to ourselves, one another, and our future generations to break the bond to money. We are the generation that is ordained to live out the true meaning of these philo-sophical metaphoric analogy of our sacred humanity. Time greets us in this moment when the humans inhabiting of this planet is out of bound. From the natural order of where we should be, living in line with the truth. Instead, we are all scattered about mentally and emotionally, unequally yoked to on abusive financial system struggling to find our way home, stuck in an environment where we are all feeling the negative effects of eating of the forbidden fruits of money, the behaviors that separate humans from truth.

Time brought greater knowledge that is calling us home together as one family. I say to all of you, these are the days we now have the eyes that see clearly and the ears that clearly hear the truth. I say to all humans in a synchronized voice, we must answer our true calling. We must not miss the opportunity to put our time together in four-hour super time slots.

Greater intelligence is making it easy for all our able-bodied men to support all their families sufficiently and efficiently by joining a noble, meaningful participation in the civic duties of a global synchronized united four-hour system. There is no greater calling and no greater power to build the proper modern infrastructures that will support new and better living conditions for all humans to enhance the life experience on every square mile of our precious planet.

Humans have the power to be good, but together as one eight-billion-member family unit, humans have superpowers to elevate conditions, behaviors, and relationships, upholding the true values and sacredness of our only planet and the many lives that depend on its healthy nourishment daily together in time molded in four-hour cubes of energy, which is where our superpower lies in wait for the wisest generation to claim.

The truth, our creator God gives humans time generously, which bring all goods to our feet, awaiting human mind to properly process and distribute without skipping a single human life. The metaphoric analogy of this wisdom is a wise man is giving ten containers of apple; he must travel the entire planet and make sure every single human being alive is fed a piece of apple. The generation who figures out how he does it is the generation that will be given paradise, "heaven," the best living condition on our planet. Humans shall not live by breath alone but by wisdom, intelligence, and knowledge from the truth. That is where humanity will hover in this circle of safety and wellness, happy and free, in mind, body, and soul, closer to the creator of life, living our best life.

Humans are species of habits. The human's nature is humans will shy away from the unfamiliar and fear what they don't understand. That's the nature of humans. We are a species with bad and good habits that are difficult to change. The truth advises humans that we all can bring out our best behaviors through time, earning positive and valuable changes in human civilization. The truth shows us a closer look at human behavior stemming from human nature. Humans like pleasant new experience, living life constantly, seeking the latest changes that would enhance a more pleasant experience in their life span. Soon those experiences become normal habits that is hard to break and discarded. That endless wrestle between human nature and human behavior is why the course of humanity is not quick or easy to change, but time brings knowledge, which gradually facilitate positive, helpful changes in human lifestyle on this planet.

Humans alive today would never give up their cell phones to go back to the pager and corner payphones. They will never give up their modern automobiles with all the latest tech and creature comforts for Henry Ford Model T. Humans today will never give up the advanced flying machines loaded with the latest navigation systems and computer technology for the Wright Brothers' Kitty Hawk Flyer. Humans are open and receptive to changes that would make their life easier and more comfortable. Optimistic and ready for change, time finds humanity here in a state of tyranny of a corrupt political system and abusive lopsided financial system. That leaves our generation in constant agony, stress, and pain.

Time brought us God's greater knowledge, which we will turn into the technologies to free ourselves from the past barbaric, uncomfortable, uninhabitable, unfair living conditions. We want you to experience our planet in new, easy, comfortable living conditions. We invite all the weary, tired, the suffering to step forward away from the old broken, primitive, throwback systems of hard and stressful living conditions to join us to form a new and improved four-hour united union, an unbreakable bond between all eight billion members of our human family. We will transform your life and living conditions on your planet to you living the good times humans will never go back from just like humans will never go back from supercomputers and cell phones, just as humans will never go back from luxurious cars, luxurious airplanes, luxurious housing, and all the creature comforts we have discovered and utilized so far.

I guarantee everyone once the humans of this generation experience living life on our planet without the misguided restrictions of the forbidden fruit, "money," we will never go back; all eyes will be open to clearly see how abusive and destructive the primitive idea of money is to the lifetimes humans spend on this planet. Unfortunately, people continuously fall for the "money trick" of gorging the forbidden fruits. Somehow the number one suspect of heinous human atrocities continues to convince humans that they cannot live good lives without its daily use.

We deserve better—a better, easier way to live like the wealthy humans that we are. Time opens revelations of truth to cut ties with the primitive past of the buying and selling ideas. We now have the knowledge, we have the technology, we have the intelligence to leap away from primitive and destructive ways of living. God's greater knowledge gave this generation the blessed light and the map to mine the ultimate power of unification through the love of the majority. Humans will never go back from the synchronization cooperation of eight billion humans united in one by a valuable four-hour labor union, operating according to the truth of human's rights. That is the sacred righteousness all humans far and wide crave, a signed contract of reassurance in the form of a four-hour worldwide labor union.

Let us help our generation, our human family, because in turn we will all get help from our fellow human beings. This speech is by no means coincidence. This speech is ordained and destined for your hearing your all-valuable members of this generation with the heightened senses to see, hear, and take the appropriate action to change the state of the human conditions, redirecting everyone's steps toward humans' best living conditions ever on our planet. Y'all were born to be placed here in this moment in this generation, to be blessed by the truth, God, the creator of our precious planet, and all that is in and on it.

Never forget that all the advances humans have made, all the new discoveries, new knowledge, innovative technologies humans utilize today were always here on our magnificent home planet Earth just patiently waiting to be discovered by us, the human generations that will grow out of adolescence and reach a more mature wisdom, the greater understanding of who humans really are? What is our true purpose? The true meaning of our existence on this planet, how far humans are on that golden ladder of humanity's life span on this planet? And even how far this planet is on the chart of its own life span?

The fact is everything, believe it or not, has an average life span. The truth suggests the nature of all life and things in our universe were first nonexistent then existent then maturity then expiration. Time is all our master. The wisest humans make the best of their time while they still see the sunshine, In its own, time will reward good with good and bad with bad. Each generation reaps the condition and behavior they plant. The sun is shining, destiny is calling, all humans within the sound of my speech. Y'all were meant to hear this call to a better life condition. We have finally figured out how to revolve around the sun at 67,000 miles per hour properly, easily, happily, wealthily, and safely, with all eight billion of us comfortably secure in our seats for the ride of our life span.

Greater intelligence gets humans all prepared to live our best life in abundance here and now in this time frame. The financial system we rely on for our ride home is broken down and leaves us all stranded and in disarray, but have no fear—we are the generation that greater change was given. The money is like a fallen angel, inefficient and insufficient with countless flaws—flaws that manipulate people into committing heinous atrocities against our human families, a disease we now can cure. The money system could never be as valuable as what we found, mining the truth. We are joined in a relentless pursuit of the best ideas on how to inhabit our planet. The dead president's idea to print the image of their faces on fabric is a failed outdated idea designed to induce and force the people's participation. This idea was destined to become a failed experiment of an immoral system. It is a system that must be locked away into the vaults of the dead. It can never even begin to approach the accomplishment we are about to achieve.

Using this generation's new ways, newly adopted digital currency, the new digital point system, "DPS," cannot be stolen. It cannot be duplicated. It cannot be cheated. In one synchronized voice and all fingerprint signed, we can all guarantee one another that every single human born to our time on this planet will have a healthy share of all daily needs and wants, greatly improving the quality of their life every day of their life span on this planet.

Once any human sees and hears this pure truth, they cannot unsee or unhear it—that is the natural checkmate for humans. Once we a find a better way for anything, we will never go back to the old way. This speech is calling you and this generation to the table of unification, to reap the prosperous benefits of being a human alive and united here and now. Join as one family, securing a true bond for you and all your offsprings now and future generations.

The truth of humanity is asking you, "by no means a coincidence," to become a member of a worldwide four-hour union—a union that will pay you and all your families cost of living for life payable with fingerprint touch-screen access to all goods and all services anywhere on our planet you happen to be. The use of this technology is the ultimate show of our power against destructive enemy behaviors on our planet. This new intelligent system is like unto bringing out billions of fighter jets for you and your families' best planet life. We will use this new intelligent power to reap the full benefits of organized caring and sharing love through real actions, advancing with the knowledge that answers the call to finally unite humans as one force on our planet, utilizing new technologies that give back humans their free time.

Once they are members of humanities four-hour work union, we will turn the hands of time to a time when only four hours a day, four days a week, nine months a year, for thirty years of civic duties will pay your way through life, keeping a simple, easy, and light work schedule that only required participation from only able-bodied men and robots as they fulfill four hours scheduled slots with enough labor time to satisfy all funding agreement as a part of a sign contract with the people made real by the people's educated awareness that this generation can, should, and will live this way of superior living conditions, enjoying their life span living easy, safe, and stress-free lives, utilizing the power of digital technology, the mathematics that continually counts you as an especially important valued member and beneficiary of human's newly found success—the success that affords our union to deliver humans everything you can ever want and need "that's legal" on this planet for all your life span courtesy of the always sufficient, always in abundance digital point system.

There is no greater call, no greater cause but to join the union that will stop human suffering and stop the shedding of innocent human blood. We must preserve the sacred sanctity of human life on every square mile of our precious home planet. Humans must immediately stop killing one another for any reason by all means necessary. People must come together to stop depicting images of humans abusing, hurting, attacking, arming, and killing humans. These types of violent images displayed in movies, songs, books, video games have extremely negative emotional effects on the human mind. It is psychological abuse, which causes serious behavioral defects that become extremely dangerous to our generation, mostly affecting the younger minds of humans.

Art imitates life, but life imitates art. We must stop portraying so much human violence in what is supposed to be entertainment. Human life is sacred, and we will uphold the sacred sanctity of human life in all our actions and behaviors toward one another planetwide. In a positive united effort, we will stop consuming human violence for entertainment. We will used God's greater sacred knowledge to get out ahead of these problems and curve all our actions that develop into negative behaviors among humans. Many generations were called to this righteous order, but our generation—this generation—has the means, the knowledge, the capacity, the intelligence to answer this emergency call. There are no parameters on what the human mind can accomplish in effort to unite all eight billion humans into our true and rightful place as one family unit on our magnificent planet. It is as easy as capturing one knowledge that had been evading human for many generations—the lack of that knowledge that the truth advice we all suffer from.

As your newly elected ordained leader, I say yes, we can, with wisdom and truth, we can finally change the human living conditions on our only planet to satisfy the needs of all eight billion and growing number of us, riding the truth at God's speeds of wealth—happy, safe, and free. I am here to inform you of better days and to guide you to your best life. Cradling the exceptional value of each human life in the average eighty years life span humans are allowed on this planet.

When the truth speaks, be humble and listen. You will do yourself and your generation well. Each human only has one life to live. Live good, and your offspring will be rewarded good, sayeth the pure truth of humankind. We must stop supporting the insanity of misguided leaders that continue to lead our generation to eat the forbidden fruits down the deadly money road. Today I say to all humans, we are going to stop following money into living conditions that gets worse day by day. Insanity is continuing to do anything repeatedly and expecting different results. Humans continue to eat of the forbidden fruit by supporting the money system and expect our conditions to change. Meanwhile, living conditions keep getting worst. The wars continue. Starvation continues. Mass shooting continues. Millions of humans are still going without proper medical attention. There is never going to be enough money to pay for all the help and attention this generation needs.

There will never be enough money to pay for the proper nutritional needs of all the people, to pay for enough doctors to treat us, enough peace officers to keep cities and homes safe. The money is not able to pay for the number of teachers we need to properly educate our most important future generation, our kids. The money's primitive system is not prepared to give all our elder humans the special comfort care they need approaching the sunset of their lives. The money falls short in all the ways people need it most. You name the need, and we can prove that we now have something better than money to fulfill humans needs. We have God's greater knowledge, the intelligence that produces fair and balanced systems that serves the needs of all eight billion of us—flawlessly, efficiently, and properly fair and balanced—a people-friendly system that guarantees your personal safety and the proper attention paid to all aspects of your average eighty-year life span.

Gods' knowledge is always greater all the time. Human minds will fail them without this superintelligence—the knowledge that the truth warns human generations will suffer without. The truth says unto human, there must not be any buying or selling anywhere on this sacred planet. God, the truth, creator of people, does not condone money. Buying and selling is a deadly sin, one of the forbidden fruits of this planet. The truth tried to teach humans a valuable lesson when the money changers were chased out from buying and selling out of the sacred temple of God. That depiction was mis-interpreted. It is the case of the victors write the history to favor their ways.

The moneychangers ruled the days of that time. They falsely interpret the truth so they can continue in the misguided ways of buying and selling what was given to humans for free. All things are given to be gathered with time and only a little sweat of the brow. The human body and mind are the sacred temple of God, our creator. The truth attempts to drive buying and selling out of the minds of human, but they disobeyed, depicting false images which mis-lead many generations of humans into buying and selling their birthrights.

Now this is our time. Our generation is ready to break the destructive cycle of money, an inefficient poor curse. The lies of misguided leadership will no longer stop humans from living in the reality that humans are not short of anything on our generously, constantly giving planet. The people are only misled into thinking they are short of money. The truth informs people you do not need money for your livelihood on your own planet. The misleading, deceptive idea of money is poisoning our generation, robbing humans' ability to enjoy their best life in their life span on our planet.

Greater intelligence gives humans the guidance to pass the forbidden ideas on to human nourishing greener ideas. We are going to revoke our consent to the money suspect responsible for the suffering of billions. Our biggest enemy is now wounded. It is time to finish it off and abolish the money. Stop eating and feeding the forbidden fruits to our family. Use greater intelligence to sign a peace treaty with all the countries that separate humans on our planet. These separations are clear marks of inferior human understanding of our one-planet dwelling—unwanted, unnecessary disruptions of people's time frame in humans' one life span for the greater good of humanity now and for all future generation.

We must act now with the strongest synchronized push and the loudest synchronized voice. All of you are chosen to be the ones at the forefront of human evolution. People are tuned in to the most powerful time and sounds of change you ever heard in your lifetime. You must not pretend that you can ever unhear the truth, calling you and your family to a life of financial weightlessness to live your life without any financial burden ever again. About every one thousand years, human evolution will thrust humanity's knowledge closer to the circle of the truth. That truth found favor in me and place me here in time in front of you, in this time frame of my generation, demonstrating that we now have the knowledge, the means, intelligence, and technology to build the metaphoric vehicle that transport humans to a type-one civilization. The time on this planet where the facts light the ways up and out of primitive failed systems where humans live super lives in timeframes of meaningful, fulfilling, and satisfied life span.

The truth transform my life, the heart of me is generous, kind, and true. My eyes can see green pastures. My ears are extremely sensitive to the suffering cries of this, my generation. My mind is elevated to the endless possibilities of a planet upgrade reunion. I decided to follow the truth home, aided with greater knowledge on loan from God. I will serve my people, my generation, my fellow human family members with all my existence.

Humans are born to our beautiful planet to serve one another as one family of many members. No one human is an island; we need one another for all things. We need for every able-bodied man of the eight billion growing numbers of us to join force in one labor time. Time has the ability to give humans all and take all. Time first held the knowledge of all technologies that we have discovered so far. Humans took a closer look at gravity and produced flight. Now our knowledge is mature enough to give us the intelligence to take a closer look at time, in which we can see lighter workloads of only four hours workdays, sixteen hours work-week, and earlier retirement times.

An even closer look at time unlocks greater knowledge of more free time, more relaxing time, and a more joyful lifetime. There is the proper knowledge in time for everything as we spend all our time traveling 67,000 miles per hour around our star sun, and we don't even feel it. Time is great to us human. Let us all do remarkable things in the time we are given on loan on this planet from the truth, God, our creator. No more wasting precious time just watching wars, just watching mass shoot-ing, just watching humans starving, watching human blood shed, just watching all the hei-nous atrocities being committed against our human family members.

We are all right here in this moment in time where I, your truly resolute leader, guarantee all of you, my fellow planet resident, that we now have the technology to trade time at greater val-ues to the tune of endless numbers transform-ing the worst of time to the best of times on this all—our miraculous home planet. Our cups will overflow with goods and services—a generous blessing from our intelligence, which will farm the most powerful synchronized worldwide four-hour labor union ever seen on our planet.

There is incredible power in the human hands when it is used together to make work light and easy for the good of eight billion peo-ple. This transforms into the super abilities to be completely generous to one another, the never-before-seen type of human generosity—the type of generosity that will give people automobiles, homes, grocery, medical care, vacations, and all the important things humans enjoy for free with little labor requirement from only able-bodied individuals and robots' program to work. Humans will have everything on this planet "that's legal" for a four-hour labor cost, the type of generosity that will meet and surpass the needs of eight billion people with ease.

With our united four-hour labor union, we will build the factories that produces all the goods for human consumption. With our incredible ability to synchronize four-hour shifts, we will provide all the services all eight billion and growing human family member will ever need for their life span on our planet. This type-one lifestyle is where our intelligence is hovering now. Let us all claim our new life, courtesy of time bringing humanity truth in the form of God's greater knowledge. God does not condone or deal with money.

Money is a humanmade disease curable with God's greater knowledge: "Give unto Caesar what is Caesar's and unto God what is God's." The truth will demolish and destroy the need for any money systems. God's natural currency is "time"—the time humans were given generously to spend helping, caring, and sharing everything with one another generously in one love mode. We are billions of beautiful, kind hearts just waiting for the environment that is conditioned and safe enough to promote love and kindness, the reflections of our true self. This has all the power any system needs to do all the things to sustain good living conditions for all human's life forever as the sun shines.

These truths are the ones that set us all free from our enemies of destructive behaviors to ourselves. We are one human family without any separations such as language or borders, skin colors, races, or any ignorant idea uninformed humans use to create divisions on our resident planet of one family. Living our true existence is the most satisfying life spans with endless rewards. The power of the truth is here now for humanity to welcome the dawn of a new age led by wise leadership guided by truth, fair and balanced, in the right principles, morals, and values that is closest to God.

As I appear before you, my mothers and fathers, my sons and daughters, my grandmothers and grandfathers, my aunts, uncles, cousins, all my immediate and extended human family members, I alert you to this especially important crossroad in time where the life preserving decision must be made in the interest of all—the eight billion growing number of us in this generation of human family on our only home planet. God, the truth, blesses this very moment in time. I thank every one of you, my human family, for answering destiny's call and choosing a new intelligent system to lead our generation.

Out of the valley of these dark shadows, onto the fruitful planes of our planet, I promise to always seek the best council from the truth. I promise to lead with wisdom, principle, and the highest morals and values. I ask all of you to be at your best morals, principles, and values, do all you can that is honest and true to help me to serve you as the best leader in the history of humanity. All things are possible in truth. With your help, I will lead this generation to prove it, to ourselves, and one another.

The only thing that subjects humans to any suffering and lack of anything on this large fruitful planet is ignorance. If there was no ignorance, this generation of humans would all have huge houses for every family unit. If there was no ignorance, there would be no homelessness nowhere on our planet. If there was no ignorance, everyone who can operate one safely would have the use of any mode of transportation. They want anywhere, anytime, from the many choices of bikes, cars, trucks, or whatever mode of vehicles humans are using—personal, recreational, and commercial vehicle—as their needs require.

If there was no ignorance, the personal safety of all humans would increase 100 percent. No ignorant humans would be able to travel the eight corners of our planet without charge or passport. No ignorance, no more wars. If there were no ignorance, humans would never kill humans for any reason, and the unborn would be safe from the attack of abortions. With this sacred knowledge, humans would immediately sign a peace treaty with the unborn because humans will never know who they are attacking in the womb.

With each attack by abortion, we are attacking one of our own that could be blessed with the greater wisdom of more abundant life for humanity. We must always protect the most innocent and most vulnerable of the sacred sanctity of life in all stages. We must always remember we all once were at that stage of life—no ignorance—and all humans on the planet would start getting the best medical and dental care constantly available on demand by touchscreen all the time of their life span, no ignorance, and humans would live life in permanently better-quality conditions on our planet, no ignorance, and the people's possibilities have no parameters.

Our generation was born for this moment and this intelligent conditioning of life spans' lifestyles. We say a prayer for past generations that were not born in time to receive this blessing, uniting for a more intelligent cohabitation of an upgraded lifestyle in your life span. We now have the true awareness of who we really are, what we are here for, and where we are going. Our generation now have the once-allusive operation manual for our planet, mind, and body. We are ready to conduct the perfect orchestra of human family synchronization produced by the most advanced technology from the highest intelligence people have ever utilized in this planet history.

We are blessed we are advanced, ready, willing, and able to move time into new dimensions where humans live in times when everything is free and the people's cost of living is eliminated by four-hour labor, a dimension of time on our planet where humans are totally free, safe, happy, and satisfied with their lives and living conditions. Thank you all for being present—now let us go! Go enjoy the fruited planes of our planet.

With that speech heard around the planet, that group of humans at the cutting edge of human evolution started building everything new. They literally threw out the old ideas on how to inhabit a planet and quickly adopted new ways to live with one another. They all started to prove to themselves and the entire planet of families. Life is easier when humans are properly positioned to conduct all the weekly tasks needed to fulfill all the demands of all life participants.

The managers assembled the teams to build all new modern roads with built-in safety feature that the new vehicles can interact with to avoid accidents. For example, they installed advanced lane monitors that guarantee that all vehicle on the roads will stay in lane unless it is safe to change. They built all the roads with interactive road signs that not just warn drivers but slow vehicles down where there is deep corner sign and stops vehicles at stop signs. They assigned a road safety team that is constantly studying the data and implementing safer changes.

They assembled the team that builds the factories that manufacture and produce all vehicles. These modern machines are built to last, with advanced self-driving artificial intelligence built in that interact with the roadway's pedestrian, other vehicles, and all objects. These semiautonomous vehicles are all 100 percent safer than the past vehicles that expose humans to so much danger daily. All the materials humans need and use to build all things come directly from the ground. It is the nature of the planet to be always giving all things to humanity.

They assembled a mining team to mine all the materials they will need to design, manufacture, and build everything—all the hardware, software, and durable goods that make all the participants' lives comfortable and easy. They assembled a team to design, manufacture, and build all the robots they will need to perform upward of 70 percent of all the labor load. They finally realized how much more they can have and get done when there is no money to hamper their efforts. They assembled a team to design and build strong long-lasting advanced homes. All these modern homes were built hurricane-, fire-, and flood-proof, with the most durable, strong materials. These new generation homes had the ability to float and aerodynamic shapes, which will withstand hurricane force winds of a category six or more. All these homes were built with the latest interactive appliances, entertainment, and furniture.

All homes were equipped with the latest creature comfort suited for the best of living conditions. All homes were self-sustained, powered with free solar and wind energy. Light bills were no more—that became the distant past life. They assembled a team to design and build the most advanced flying machines ever used by humans. These airplanes, helicopters, and flying crafts were all amphibious with redundancy safety measures. All these aircrafts were all built with advanced safety features that is designed to avoid crashes and save lives. All these crafts were all built with double backup engines and are designed to land anywhere on land or water, assuring there is no loss of human life in the event of an emergency.

They made all human travel 100 percent safer on land, air, and sea—a great testament to the advanced safety measures of all vehicles humans use for travel. Deadly crashes quickly became a thing of their past. They assembled a team to design and build all schools as interactive learning centers, then they staffed all those schools with the proper staffing at the right teacher to student ratios to ensure that all kids get the proper attention each one needs. These types of attention paid to their kids from early childhood will ensure favorable behaviors in their future in human society. This type of forward planning and advanced designs of human's education systems will eliminate future misbehaviors and crimes.

They established modern learning institutes that train and graduate their most intelligent doctors, biologists, scientists, engineers, psychologists, and all the expertise needed to lift human society upward, focusing on the best interest of humanity all at an easy, shared four-hour labor cost. All these trained professionals took an ethical oath to do no harm and always be true to all humans doing their best for humanity's best interest. They went to work to ensure all humans stay healthy, wealthy, comfortable, and safe, developing new medicines to aid and cure diseases. They went on the offensive looking out for any illness that might become epidemic or pandemic, developing medication, equipment, regiments, and curricula to keep their generation strong and healthy mentally and physically. With their actions and behaviors, they were proving that there is no perimeter to what humans can and will do for one another when there is no money in the way to hamper their efforts.

They assembled a team that is responsible for the proper nutrition of all the participants. These humans' duties are to farm, store, and distribute all food to everyone with the option of delivery, cooked or uncooked, by way of one of the most advanced ordering apps via the cell phone which was given to everyone for free with no phone bill. They were doing wonders to make living easy for all, and it started showing in people's behavior toward one another.

Humans were starting to interact differently with their neighbors. Their speech was more friendly, and their behavior was kind. Humans were happier with their easier living conditions. They were quickly removing the stress from human living. They were proving the facts of human nature when they provide a peaceful, stress-free, comfortable living environments for all humans. They noticed big positive changes in human behavior toward one another and the very systems that sustain those conditions. Now they were quickly perfecting living arrangements, jobs, transportation, medical attention, food distribution, water dispensation, electric power sustainment. They were relentless in their quest to provide all the necessities for the highest quality of living condition.

To honor the lives of all the participants in this extremely important test run—a test run that will pave golden ways to humans finally seeing and recognizing one another with the sense of family in love—they were securing the best conditions for optimum behavior. They forbade any deliberate action by anyone that would cause negative behaviors in human society. This intelligent system virtually eliminates robberies, murders, racism, and all human suffering. They called a meeting with the entertainment community, the leaders and psychologists assigned to the acceptable entertainment committee. They informed all artists, moviemakers, video game designer, songwriters, and all authors. The entertainment rules had changed; there must be no books, songs, plays, movies, video games, or any form of media depicting any disrespectful, violent, devious, dishonest, ratchet, or barbaric behaviors toward fellow humans. Studies show depicting negative images and negative behaviors of their human families is very toxic for all humans especially the children. The truth points out that what is bad for the children is a huge problem for future humans.

At the cutting edge of human evolution, greater knowledge sees that violence saturating entertainment eventually becomes violent saturating human society in their homes, their streets, their countries. Humans now realize that it's more valuable to behave in more favorable ways to one another. These positive and favorable behavior in human society makes people a much more valuable commodity to themselves and one another. They study the cause of a problem and get out ahead of the problem to curve behaviors for more positive results. It is a win for all, bringing humans into better positions to properly serve their generations on that planet.

With all the participants now living in modern homes with no bills or payment, they all enjoyed those living arrangements without the stress of owning. They loved the fact that they can just occupy an assigned house anywhere on the planet they choose as a part of an extensive network of house in a giant timeshare system. All maintenance and repairs are free, courtesy of the united four-hour green union—the union that is always fully staffed with members of able-bodied men and robots ready to perform all official labor for everyone. The system only requires work from robots and able-bodied men for an easily maintained schedule of four hours per day, four days per week, nine month per year.

Wisdom, technology, and humans' willingness to work together produce this incredibly valuable synchronized four-hour labor force. This type of organization is performing daily miracles in the lives of billions of humans. Everyone loved that easy conditioned lifestyle they were now enjoying. People will never go back to inferior living conditions. People will never go back to bearing the burden of providing the needs of their family alone when now it is so much easier and simple with the help of billions of humans living and working together as one family unit—all with one and all humans' best interest in mind always.

The times and days when humans seek to do things without the proper assistance is past and gone, never to return. Humans now have access to vast networks of people, robots, and technology to provide enormous quantities of goods and services at the accurate numbers and ratios the human species require daily on that rich planet. This generation is the one that is now grown out of adolescence and primitive ways to higher realizations to now mining the riches of unification. They now can see that they were always rich as their planet stayed fruitful and provided all their needs. They now totally understand that they can only suffer arm from their biggest enemy—"ignorance." They now have the refined intelligence to pinpoint the enemies that lie, deceive, and divide them. They now can isolate and surgically remove the actual and metaphorical diseases that ails them. Now they all know that their greatest power lies within their ability to unite as one—one for all, all for one—out of many humans are one.

The bond of eight billion humans is the sacred truth; this must never be broken. It is the power and strength humans need to overcome all the obstacles to people's best life on their planet from cradle to grave. All around the island, humans are pleased and amazed. There are bursting in excitement and joy at all the new things they can now do as part of new lifestyle conditioning. Everything they need and use is now easy to get. Life is easy and worry-free, knowing that they are now living in an advanced intelligent human society. Modern people that take the time to give the best total care to one another throughout their entire life span on their generous planet.

Human suffering has quickly become a thing of the past. Now humans just inhabit the island, enjoying the beauty of each day made even more beautiful with the facts of their reality now. When they want a house, they can get one with several options to choose from at the house marts in a couple of hours. When they need a vehicle, all who has a license could fingerprint sign one out from one of the many auto marts in a few minutes. No charge, just a touch of their fingerprint to register the use of any object—vehicles, equipment, houses—whatever humans need and use. If they have the proper license to operate one safely, they can have the use of it all at no charge.

When they need food, they can order pickup or delivery, prepared or unprepared, from one of the many food marts that's always fully stocked with all food humans eat courtesy of the best farming and food distribution team ever assembled in the history of man. The latest technology makes getting food easy for everyone on a cell phone app that takes delivery and pickup orders twenty-four hour a day at no charge. When they want clothes, they shop from online clothing apps for what they like for pickup or delivery from one of the many clothes marts courtesy of the team in charge of fashion, making, distributing, and recycling all garments for all members of the human's family—all sizes, styles, age, and purpose—no charge because the pay arrangements are all prepaid by their massive four-hour union.

Living in this condition, all are wondering what took so long to get their planet in that mode of greater conditions of life. Men over fifty are all retired with full benefits for as long as their life spans. Kids under twenty are being educated by the best education systems—truly no child left behind because the teacher-student ratio is excellent. There are enough teachers to take time and make time with each child according to their individual need. The throwback money ignorance could not pay for such attention to all their precious commodity of human children.

The children love this new system; they all feel the sense that they are becoming a part of a system that is guaranteeing them everything they will need for their life journey, a system that helps them to become valuable, important, and special members of a loving human family, a system that's proving to people that the more they work together, the more efficiently everyone gets fed, clothed, sheltered in premium living conditions. They see their older siblings becoming valuable, prominent members of a more intelligent future human society. They're seeing a system that's making them excited and proud to become a part of. They also like the fact that they only attend school four hours a day, four days a week, nine months a year.

Humans now realize if they take the pressure off the children and give them more resources, they will perform better in school and in life, securing a better future for humanity. The women are the happiest from this signed agreement. They are free from any official labor schedule. Women do not have to work; they are all free to follow their own natural schedule. The women have all the free time they need to address the things that are naturally important to them and their immediate and extended family. The old saying "If the women are happy, the whole family is happy" is proving itself to be true. God's greater knowledge point out the facts—women and men are made differently, biologically and mentally enhanced to become an equal part of one, each with their own super ability that can never be successfully transferred. In fact, when one is imitated by the other, it leads to disaster in the human family structure.

The bond between man and woman was established not to be broken. From the beginning of human's time on that planet, human man and woman need each other. They got each other because they belong together to form one rich and happy united family state. Men and women are the best two parts of a beautiful life in a human life span of living their best only "one life." The roughly four billion women on that planet are rejoicing because they helped men to design a system that guarantees their exemption from work—a system that gives them more free time and complete freedom with touchscreen digital funs. Humans can all see from here life is going to be 1,000,000 percent better for people—both women and men—when men and women are joined in a sacred matrimony force, following humanity's true knowledge of love.

*Love* the word becomes the philosophy that breeds innovative technology—tech that supports the true ambitions that gives humanity back all things on their planet, all free, through touch-screen digital funs, acknowledging and utilizing the sacred birth-right of all humans born of planet Earth, using advanced intel-ligence to live life free, knowing that out of many, there is only one human family. The increase of knowledge evolves a more intelligent love for humanity. That intelligence of love is the power that will steer time dimension to creating the most ideal, healthy, wealthy, comfortable, intelligently appropriate living conditions for all of humanity.

All age groups, male and female, participating in the test run are happy with the results—results that are proving that it is easy to abolish money by no longer embracing the main suspect—the primitive idea of money that is directly and indirectly responsi-ble for billions of humans' bloodshed, pain, and suffering. It's a primitive exchange of goods and services that's robbing people daily from their God-given sacred birthright to enjoy living a safe, happy, meaningful, rich life span on their miraculous planet Earth. It is the moments in time when help is always available for real use-ful assistants to all humans in signed contracts, releasing female from labor and financial burden and giving all people sufficient help taking care of their families guaranteed by the massive masses of the people's intelligent united worldwide four-hour labor-union that is now providing all the resources needed to remove God's true people from any financial restrictions for the duration of their average eighty years' life span, transforming the ways they live out their daily lives to a time on that planet where human life is free from primitive levels of ignorance, free from the dangerous lack of knowledge which facilitate the pillaging of their generation times. Now everyone is taking their place in the new advanced system with greater knowledge, more intelligence, greater self-aware-ness—the intelligence that is in a relentless pursuit of a type-one civilization.

Just one taste of these ways, no human can go back to living a primitive life in a primitive use of time, operating in times when human generations are decaying. In the state of lies, deceptions, gluttony, greed, hate, jealousy, envy, it goes on—the devil's and forbidden fruits of humanity. Superintelligent behaviors give humans the antidote knowledge that surgically extract all misguided, counterproductive behaviors from human society. Humans now have the knowledge to utilize and maximize time by spending no time on counterproductive behaviors to spending all time on only productive behaviors. They are now signing contracts that guarantees all humans born on that planet will be given optimum care from the unborn to their sunset on that planet.

They are now employing intelligence that is conquering humans and animal illness with leaps in advanced medical tech. They are conquering daily living arrangements with much more convenient housing. That are engineered stronger and safer, fire and storm proof, with self-sustaining power sources of green solar and wind energy. They are fulfilling the proper nutritional needs of their generation. They are acknowledging "you are what you eat" and making sure they research and produce the most nutritional food. They are employing the most advanced farming technology that produces and stores enough healthy food year-round to feeding all appetites, available to everyone through one of the many strategically placed food marts. Advanced food distribution supported by the latest technology that synchronize the coordination of robots and humans are always ready for pickup or delivery, cooked or uncooked. The only problem humans have with food in this time is learning the discipline not to overeat. They are using interactive roads and vehicles with artificial intelligence, semiautonomous vehicles that interact with the roads and its surrounding, making traveling on land 1,000 percent safer than past primitive, dangerous ways of traveling on land. They are building all new flying machines with redundancy safety measures that guarantee there will never be a deadly crash. All flying crafts are now amphibious and can switch between manual or autonomous mode. They can take off and land almost anywhere on water or dry land. They are quickly improving all aspects of humans' living conditions on that island.

Starting on that upgrade island, they are laying rock-solid foundations, which will serve the dawn of a new age in time on that planet. They are all dedicated to giving their planet a well-needed upgrade. They are changing the rules of human engagement across that island. They are teaching themselves priceless, lasting values—the best way to use advanced technologies aided by reprogrammable robots to producing all the resources needed to sustain all the people's needs and wants. They are seducing time to create a new environment where humans coinhabit their home planet in superintelligent mode. They are teaching people new communication skills in one language—the type of skills that give people their best life. They now utilize the intelligent skill sets that make all work light and easy. They are now using the latest in robot technology to perform 70 percent of all workloads. They are enjoying times when robots are programed to be faithful partners to all people, making all aspect of that planet life more satisfying for humanity. They continue to improve on human behaviors toward one another to the level of making every one life span healthier, wealthier, and safer. Humans are using their latest intelligence to make their life spans value more to one another.

The buzz of the upgrade island is spreading all over the planet. It has been four years since the trial run started. The rest of the planet wants to know—are people happier? Is life easier? Are living conditions much better? Is that type of living more in tune with the nature of humans? All those questions must be answered. That was the job of the reporters that was sent from countries around the planet. All the reporters fan out across the upgrade island. They are interviewing several participants to get the real story and the true answer to the biggest question—is this lifestyle a more valuable option?

A reporter interviews a sixteen-year-old boy.

The reporter asks the boy, "How is the new system treating you?"

The boy responded, saying, "I love my life. I'm in school for only four hours a day. The rest of the time, I spend enjoying one of my many hobbies with my age-group friends—like this afternoon, me and some of my age-group friends are going to hit one of the best dirt bikes track ever built. Yes, and the best part is we never have to pay for the use of the bikes. We just must follow safety rules, and everything we need is touchscreen sign out sign in. I just turn sixteen, and after taking and passing all the safety driving courses, I get my license, and now I can drive on the roads. I feel happy that I have access to a variety of different type of vehicles. The new system makes it so easy for a young boy like me to drive a nice vehicle for free. Whenever me and my peers need the use of a car, we just go to one of the many car marts and fingerprint sign one out. If we always drive safe and follow the rules, we have that privilege for life."

The reporter asks, "What would you like to be?"

The boy responds, "You mean what position I want to play in the four-hour work union?"

The reporter said, "Yes."

The boy said, "Well, I would like to work building and maintaining robots. I'm very happy that the new four-hour system will educate me and train me for jobs in the four-hour labor union at no cost. The new system is taking the worry and uncertainty from my future. The new system is guaranteeing me everything on this planet I need or want that's legal. As long as I uphold my end of the contract by performing my four-hour duties, four-hours a day, four days a week, nine months a year for thirty years starting at age twenty, retired at age fifty, the four-hour system signs a contract with me that guarantees me enough digital fun to be wealthy for my life span. That is a great solid, easy, safe, fair, quality life and future for me with plenty of free time between work time and retire time to live and enjoy my best life stress-free. I am looking forward to enjoying a better-quality life span. I love and appreciate the highly intelligent teamwork of my generation as one human family."

The reporter said, "Thank you for your time. Sounds like you're in for a bright future."

Another reporter interviewed a young lady, age twenty-four, that's in her third month of pregnancy.

The reporter asks, "What is it like being pregnant in this new system?"

The young lady responds, "I feel great and very excited about my baby coming into the world at a time when pregnant women have all the assistance and help they need. From the moment I find out I was pregnant, I was assigned a personal nurse and a personal doctor to attend to all me and my baby's needs plus all the help and attention I'm getting from my immediate and extended family who now have more free time to spend helping me. One of the best parts is all this medical attention don't cost me anything. I'm very pleased with the high-quality attention they've been paying to me and my babies' health. I'm also very excited and looking forward to spending my time raising my child without ever having to work a job. I love the advanced intelligent labor system that declares women don't have to work any official jobs while being fully funded for life with enough digital fun to keep me and my kids living rich for our life span courtesy of able-bodied man intelligently putting their time together in a synchronized four-hour labor union. This new system feels like green energy for highly intelligent humans that live in abundance—safe and free. I feel such peace of mind that me and my child will never want for anything for our entire life span if we're a part of this new system."

The reporter asked her, "Do you want to have a boy or a girl?"

She said, "It really don't matter—boy or girl—either one will be welcome by me and all my extended family. We all will be glad to have him or her to become a valuable new important member of this new family system. I'm happy that the plan laid out in this new system for the kid's future is to build an environment with the infrastructure needed to nurture a successful life—safe and healthy, free from crime and poverty. It's very important to young mothers like me that our kids are heading for a future that they 99.9 percent guarantee to become successful, valuable members of their generation. All the new mothers I talk to are pleased with the new odds of their kid's success in the future."

The reporter said, "I'm amazed at your excitement and optimism about the prospect of your child's future in this new system."

The young lady said, "Yes! Because everyone seems to be sporting new social intelligence that makes it so much easier and highly hospitable for women and children in these times."

The reporter responded, "It sounds like you are getting all the help you will ever need to raise a brilliant child."

The reporter said, "Thank you, ma'am! It seems like you're ready and able, like only a woman can, to produce intelligent new members of our future human society."

Another reporter interviewed a fifty-year-old man. The reporter asks this man, "What is it like to be one of the first batch of retiree from this new system?"

The gentle man said, "It feels great. I'm loving the fact that I didn't have to work until I was sixty-five or seventy years old. I'm happy to be a part of a new system finally—a system that carefully consider s the life span of humans. Now the system is not working people till they are elderly and drop dead. The average human life span is about eighty years. The old system forces people to work eight to twelve hours a day until they are up in their sixties, seventies, eighties, elderly and weak. With the constantly rising cost of living, it has more senior citizens working way beyond the average years they should be working. I personally believe it's elderly abuse to have elders struggling with financial difficulty and insufficient medical attention. I'm enjoying the new intelligence of human society that guarantee to take the best care of all elders. I'm delighted that human civilization finally reached this stage that we are employing a system that works harder for us instead of us working harder for a system. This new system is there for people every step of their life. I retire at fifty, and now I have plenty of time to enjoy the rest of my life span while am still strong and healthy enough to live life, worry-free in financial weightlessness. I must say this past two years are the best years of my life. The living conditions are beautiful, people are more intelligent, caring and sharing. I feel like I'm a part of a huge family that really care s about my wellbeing—a family that has the means to help me with whatever my need may be, easy, with no red tape or hassle."

The reporter asks, "How do you think this new system will take care of all your daily necessity for the rest of your life span?"

The man said, "Well, because we don't use money anymore, we are reaping 100 percent on our labor time. The new advanced digital point system union is intelligent and well equipped to maximize the labor time of people and robots, making the labor time put into the four-hour union 1,000 percent more valuable to every one life. This new synchronized united labor force using digital points instead of primitive money gives people the privilege of being born wealthy and staying wealthy throughout their life span on our beautiful planet. This system employs the ability to make everything people need and want easily accessible by touch screen digital currency used to access all goods and services on the island from one of the many marts strategically placed for the most convenience—a high-quality system that uses highly advanced algorithms to anticipate the needs of all the people. We have everything humans need and use prestage and prepared for delivery or pickup from one of the many distribution marts strategically placed according to the proper ratio of the people's population because everything is designed, manufactured, and produced by the four-hour labor union. All people participating are never short of anything. It's just easy living for all age groups guaranteed by the united four-hour united labor union of the people, by the people, for the people. We should have already employed a system like this years ago, but I'm so happy and feel a sense of relief to be a part of humanity in this blessed generation times."

The reporter said to this gentleman, "With living life made this easy and worry-free with guaranteed financial security, personal safety, and unlimited care, I know what I'm going to be doing after this."

The man asks, "What?"

The reporter replied, "I'm going to become a part of this great new system. I sure would like to become a part of something meaningful, highly intelligent, and advanced for the greater good of humanity."

All the reporters went about the upgrade island, asking all types of questions in order to bring back an accurate depiction of life in the new system. The leaders on upgrade island are all very pleased with the results of the trial run so far. They notice the huge changes in people's attitude toward one another and toward the system. They are proving that if you put humans into a better environment, their behavior toward one another will greatly improve. They are engaging one another in more intelligent ways daily; they're working together more efficiently. Women and men have much more time available to raising their children to become superintelligent members of human society.

They notice with the advanced educational system and the fact that mothers don't have to work, the kids are getting more needed attention. The kids are becoming superstars, proving how much more valuable they are in this new system. They noticed that women are not opting for abortions anymore because they have all the support they could ever need taking care of their children. Raising a child in this system is so much easier than the old system. They notice all pregnant women are pleased with all the endless care they all have access to medically, physically, emotionally, financially. They notice the elderly care has improved dramatically. All elderly is now receiving the highest levels of quality care daily as needed. They notice the daily interaction between people is very productive, intelligent, and sophisticated. They notice the extra attention paid to early childhood development education now having huge effect on the kid's future. None is being lost to a life of crime. All are becoming productive members of society, taking the torch on to even better times in humanity.

They notice the new transportation system is becoming more responsive and efficient to the needs of the people, whether land, air or water, personal or public traveling. People are commuting faster and safer. They notice emergency response teams are quicker and more efficient to the needs of the people. They notice that human life overall is elevated to higher levels of living conditions. They notice times are happier and people more cooperative for the greater good of one and all. They notice that having all goods and services for the entire population staged and ready for dispense twenty-four hours a day, seven days a week, 365 days per year—these readily available necessities make life joyful to live, worry-free, with just a touch screen sign out or sign in of all things.

The digital point system backed by the four-hour labor force is a big hit with the people. The leaders and the people of upgrade island are proud and happy with the results of their efforts. The word is getting out—the idea of the new system is making perfect sense and spreading. People are becoming more receptive to the newly released truth. People having all necessity at their fingertips at all the times of their life span is an amazing blessing to every one lifestyle. With these type of high quality, fruitful, intelligent living conditions lead humans' minds to never go back to a primitive utilization of time. God is the planet's truth that gives the wisdom, which create superintelligence, knowledge that will eliminate the people's cost of living on their free planet. People all over the planet is getting anxious to try this new style system. The idea of employing a system that provides all goods and services to upgrade the lives of upward of eight billion people, staff by billions of robots and able-bodied men, is becoming more attractive each day. People from all over the different countries on their planet is becoming intrigued by this new system.

The rest of the people want to know if science fiction is really becoming science reality. They are all hearing of a healthy, fruitful, and efficient new system uniquely programmed to take full advantage of artificial intelligence to perform over 70 percent of all workloads to the aid of the people. They are sending the heads of states, prime ministers, presidents, and all kind of leaders from countries all over the planet. They all want to take a closer look at the system's performance for the people. Most of them are calling this new system the best thing since the discovery of electricity and computer chips. The people all over the planet is hungry for something new, and it is showing bright and clear in their heightened interest. The rest of the human world is envisioning planet lives' conditions, quickly advancing to higher levels and suitable dimensions—qualities of human lives that experience all thing in great abundance for their life span. They are witnessing the birth of human's superintelligent society, the early construction of the road humanity will use to relentlessly pursue a type-one civilization.

The upgrade island is symbolizing the stabilization of humanity's future by employing advanced people-friendly intelligence that is performing excellence for the good of the people, changing the whole dynamic of human existence on their loving superplanet, inducing the applause, amazement, and consent of over 98 percent of the planet's population.

The truth is out and can never be denied its rightful place in the people's lives. Their world is observing the nature of this new four-hour system, is extremely generous and attentive to all the people, utilizing intelligence that's signing lucrative contracts with the people, guaranteeing them a wealthy, safe, premium quality life span. The entire planet has all eyes on upgrade island, watching and learning the new system that will soon upgrade all their life spans—the system that's coming to the rescue of people from the atrocities of insufficient funds and poverty lifestyles. The leaders and reporters of several different countries all swarm upgrade island to observe this new system in action. Wherever they look, they notice people are responding positively to this new system. They notice people are more in tune with themselves and their reality. They are more intelligent, efficient, and cooperative with one another and the new system. They all see that when people don't have to compete for life necessities, it makes everyone enjoy a more satisfying life span—from the babies to the elderly, the truth spoke and turn word into better living conditions for the people's needs.

Across the planet, the buzz is getting louder. Everyone wants to try this new four-hour system. The microwave generation wants to live this way now, but a better-quality life takes time. Responding to the call of their constituents, the leaders all decided in one unified commitment to their people. They all decided to secede a quarter of each of their countries to become autonomous zones for the trial run of this new system that the world can't stop talking and buzzing about.

All the 195 countries on the planet decided to participate in these trial runs, designating a quarter of each country to an autonomous zone dedicated to the trial run of the brand-new four-hour system. All the people on that planet were optimistic, happy, and excited. Help for everyone has arrived. The human species is evolving quickly into a system that's clearly less stressful, safer, richer, and more comfortable, securing the well-being of human's life spans and all the lifeforms on their ever-faithful miraculous planet. They're now spreading superior intelligence to the minds of all people, giving everyone the assistance and guidance they all need to become the absolute best version of themselves, guaranteeing that their planet will become the dwelling place of superintelligent humans' lovefest—forever until the end of time.

www.ingramcontent.com/pod-product-compliance
Lightning Source LLC
Chambersburg PA
CBHW070932120626
46546CB00004B/1393